Mary Hartwell Catherwood

The White Islander

Mary Hartwell Catherwood

The White Islander

ISBN/EAN: 9783744708739

Printed in Europe, USA, Canada, Australia, Japan

Cover: Foto ©Thomas Meinert / pixelio.de

More available books at **www.hansebooks.com**

THE WHITE ISLANDER

"THEY ARE MY OWN FLOWER."

THE
WHITE ISLANDER

BY

MARY HARTWELL CATHERWOOD

AUTHOR OF "THE ROMANCE OF DOLLARD,"
"THE LADY OF FORT ST. JOHN," ETC.

NEW YORK
THE CENTURY CO.
1893

Copyright, 1893, by
MARY HARTWELL CATHERWOOD

THE DE VINNE PRESS.

PREFACE

THE Island of Mackinac, set in the most translucent waters on this continent, with Huron on one side of it and Michigan on the other, greatly fascinates both tourist and student. No landscape-gardening and placarding of commercial man can ever quite spoil its wild beauty. The white cliffs and the shaggy wilderness defy him. Across the strait, westward, is St. Ignace, where Father Marquette's grave may yet be seen, though the birch-bark coffin holding his bones has been removed to another shrine. On every anniversary of the removal, the Manito of the island remembers that despoiling, and never fails to bring a storm on the lakes. Across the strait, southward, on the mainland, the site of Fort Michilimackinac may easily be found. An irregular excavation, a scattered orchard and clusters of gooseberry-bushes, a long stretch of deep yellow sand, and the eternal glitter of the lake, remain from the old tragedy.

Skull Rock is yet known on the island as Henry's Cave. A venerable islander, Mr. Cable, told me he had found skulls there in his boyhood.

Through French, British, and early American occupation, Mackinac was the center of the fur trade. Indians and traders met here. The crescent bay swarmed with strange figures, and packs of beaver were carried from canoe to warehouse, the traffic of a continent and the result of a year's labor being disposed of in a few brief days. The American Fur Company had its headquarters at Mackinac, and living islanders— Dr. Bailey and James Lasley — can tell much of the life it annually brought to break in one great wave upon the strip of beach. You might close your eyes when the moon is large over the summer lakes, and almost hear again the roaring song of *coureurs de bois* around the turn of the bay.

ILLUSTRATIONS

                                      PAGE

"THEY ARE MY OWN FLOWER"............Frontispiece

"AN INDIAN GIRL STOOD THERE WITH A BLANKET IN HER HANDS"............................ 5

WAWATAM.. 41

"BUT NO PRIEST CAN BE A HUSBAND"........... 109

"FATHER JONOIS WAS BEGINNING THE MARRIAGE SERVICE"..................................... 153

CONTENTS

PART I

	PAGE
FORT MICHILIMACKINAC	1

PART II

THE GHOST-FLOWER 36

PART III

THE RIFT IN THE ISLAND 80

PART IV

THE HIGH PLATEAU 127

THE WHITE ISLANDER

PART I

FORT MICHILIMACKINAC

THE young fur-trader, Alexander Henry, sat in his house within the fort, writing letters. The June day was sultry. Such midsummer heat was rarely felt on the straits where the great lakes mingled.

The Chippewa Indians of the settlement were playing a game of baggatiway with some neighboring Sacs, and as they pursued the ball across half a mile of sandy beach from one post to the other, their shouts approached or retreated. The fortress gates stood open, officers and soldiers lounging outside to watch the game. Henry could see the expanse of sparkles which Lake Michigan spread beyond the palisade tips. Fort Michilimackinac was one of the oldest out-

posts of civilization on the continent. The
earliest explorers had rested here; and now
that French rule was giving way before the
pressure of England, this post grudged itself
to the new colors hanging from the flagstaff.
It had never been strongly built, having only
wooden bastions and palisades, and it had
never been so carelessly guarded as on this
June day.

Within the area, and against eastern walls,
which gave them shadow, sat Chippewa
squaws, huddling their blankets around them
in spite of the heat. There was a canoe at
the beach, just arrived from Detroit, and the
trader made haste to finish his letters that he
might go out and inquire the news of the
English garrison there. His habit of self-
control kept him at his task while the whole
settlement played.

A trampling rush of the Indians driving
their ball to the post nearest the fort came
like a sudden rustle of the lake against its
beach. Out of this noise rose another, echo-
ing from the pine-woods back of the clearing,
and filling the sky's hollow and the lake's
plane. It was the Indian war-whoop, and
meant death to the garrison.

Henry sprang to his feet, and seized his rifle, expecting to hear the drum-call to arms. But the savages took the fort in an instant. Not an English voice was raised except in death-cries. The squaws threw back their blankets, revealing the weapons they had carried into the inclosure, and gave these to the swarming Chippewas. Half-naked figures, their rigid sinews working like lines of fire, struck down and scalped all they met in their furious courses. The earth seemed turned to a frightful picture, and incredible things were done where a deceitful tribe had just been amusing themselves and their victims with ball-play.

That long moment of waiting for the signal of defense blanched the young trader. It was useless for him to take up arms alone against four hundred Indians. He saw through his open windows more than one soldier struggling between buckskin knees. The first savage eye turned his way would mark him for its next victim. The Canadians of the fort stood by unhurt, looking at the destruction of the English, as trees appear to rise calmly above a flood which they cannot stop, but which does not sweep them away. That kindness between French and aboriginal blood, which grew from century to century, was strongest at this very time. The French settlers were not to be included in the massacre.

Lake Michigan sparkled. The hot sunshine lay unchanged and serene on a turf soaking pools of scarlet, and on bodies outstretched or doubled upon themselves in heaps. Henry was conscious of perfume from the garden outside the palisades. Bees were stooping to gooseberry-bushes or searching the apple-boughs. A water-freshened breeze came upon the land, stirring foliage, while seventy men were being hacked down by six times as many savages. The gun sank in the trader's grasp. He looked around for some hiding-place. As soon as the savages left off slaughter for sacking, his storehouse would be their first thought. He could not escape through the palisades to the woods. Langlade's cottage stood next to his. The French family were gathered safely within, and it flashed through Henry that they might mercifully hide him. He had reached his back door, when it opened, and an Indian girl stood there with

"AN INDIAN GIRL STOOD THERE WITH A BLANKET IN HER HANDS."

a blanket in her hands. She was Langlade's slave, whose name her owners never took the trouble to pronounce. They called her Pani, from her tribe. Her copper skin had not its usual tint, the grayness of extreme anxiety clouding it. Pani had often come into the storehouse, and stood looking at the trader. She wore silver bands riveted on her naked ankles. Her rounded arms were bare. Only that morning, when the sun showed the crimson of her cheeks, Henry had noticed that she was handsomer than the girls of the northern tribes; but he saw her now as the means of escape. Pani beckoned to him, and threw the blanket over his head. The trader knew he was stumbling on the low fence, and then within Langlade's door. It was a back room into which Pani took him, and she pushed him up a staircase. The mob's howling filled every crevice of earth and sky that sound could penetrate.

They reached the attic. The Indian girl looked at him earnestly before she closed the attic door, shaking her head when he whispered his thanks. The young man heard her draw the key from the lock as she turned it, and her moccasins went down-stairs without his knowledge. She had put him out of the massacre for as long a time as his hiding-place would conceal him. There were no windows in this roof-room, but Henry found a crevice between timbers through which he could look into the fort. Chippewa voices were already raising the shout, "It is done!" Some half-naked fellows ran, knife in hand, toward the storehouse. At the same instant he heard others breaking into the room below.

Langlade's house had nothing but a layer of boards between lower rooms and attic. Distinctly the guttural inquiry rose through loosely covered joists:

"Are any English hiding in this house?"

"I do not know of any," replied the Frenchman.

"Where, then, is the trader?"

"You can search for him if you think he is here, and satisfy yourselves."

The man in the attic stood up and looked around him. There was a feather-bed on the floor, and in one corner were some birch-bark vessels and troughs used in making maple sugar, and during their season of disuse piled at one end of the floor under the low rafters.

Henry crept to the heap and inserted himself feet foremost. He could hear the crowding of moccasins on the narrow stairs as he labored. Water stood in chill drops on his face. He dared not disturb the light birch boxes too vigorously, for fear they would fall with a clatter, or raise suspicious dust in the air. Indians have many senses beside sight. They shook the locked door, and bumped it with their hatchets, until the key was handed up from below. Then four light-footed searchers came into the room.

Henry was scarcely concealed. His breath stopped. He expected to be seized and dragged from the heap instantly, and closed his eyes to his fate. Buckskin legs trod around in the darkness of the attic, kicking the pile, and twice brushing against him. The boxes rattled, but did not fall apart. The exhilarated savages talked of what they had done, and stood counting the number of scalps they had taken. Their search was rapid and careless. They trod on the feather-bed, and prodded the darkest corners with their hatchets. They went down-stairs, still talking, obligingly locking the door again before returning the key.

The trader crept out to the feather-bed and lay down, exhausted by suspense. His body relaxed, and he fell soundly asleep.

When he awoke it was as black as midnight in the attic, and rain was beating the bark roof over his head. The tinkling and the rush of streams down irregular grooves soothed him. It was one of those moments between perils when a fugitive rests, indifferent to his pursuers. He could hear the storm roaring on the lake. He knew it was washing away blood-stains in the fort, and perhaps quenching to sullen smoke fires which the Indians would be sure to start. Their voices in drunken cries at intervals struck across the monotone of the storm. Casks of liquor were long ago rolled out from the fort's stores. In the rain, or under shelter of barracks or officers' quarters, the victors were sprawling and drinking.

Henry sat up and looked at his hopeless case. He was probably the only living Englishman in Fort Michilimackinac. It was four hundred miles to Detroit, the nearest point of safety. If the door were unlocked, or if he could make an opening in the roof and steal out unseen as far as the beach, and find a canoe, he had nothing with which to stock it; and the whole route lay through hostile tribes who were evidently united in rising against the English. Yet to stay was to die. The Indians knew him well. They owed him for goods. By morning they would search him out, and as many as could unite in paying him with their hatchets would cut him down.

His troubled thoughts, and the downpour on the roof, must have shut his ears to noise in the room below; for he was startled at seeing a rod of light appear under the attic door. By this token Henry knew a candle was coming up-stairs.

Monsieur Langlade was the bearer of it.

"You searched the place yourselves," he said outside the door, his key groping for its bolt in the lock. "Very good. Look again. Look until you are satisfied."

The door swung back, and Monsieur Langlade stepped in, lifting his candle so that its sheen fell upon naked red heads and shoulders gorging the staircase.

The young trader stood up. His person expanded, and he fixed an unmoving eye on the rabble. As Monsieur Langlade's candle revealed the occupant of the attic, he uttered a nervous cry. It was for the children asleep below, rather than for the trader, whose concealment in his house might bring vengeance on them. He had himself so many times braved death with coolness that it did not seem to him the worst thing which could befall a man, but it was a pitiable thing for the very young.

The foremost savage caught Henry by the collar, and lifted his knife. Death was endured in that action, though the raised arm was not permitted to inflict it. A Chippewa in hunting-dress caught the knife-handle.

The little yellow flame scarcely showed two struggling figures, or the faces brought close together by the bracing of sinewy limbs. Other Indians poured into the attic, but waited, weapons in hand, respecting the brief wrestle of the two for the knife. In the midst of this effort made for him, Henry was conscious that a mouse squeaked in a corner, and he saw the heap of birch-bark troughs enlarging and contracting in the weird play of light. Imperfect as was his knowledge of the Chippewa tongue, he seized the meaning of the fierce words between the holders of the knife.

"Will you kill my adopted brother before my eyes?" The hunter was Wawatam. Henry knew his voice.

"We will make broth of all the English."

"But every man in the tribe promised me to save the life of my brother, if I would go away and not tell him. I went."

"We know that well. We know Wawatam went hunting, instead of lifting the hatchet against the English. The fort at Detroit is taken, and all the tribes are risen with Pontiac to sweep the English from our country. And Wawatam goes hunting."

"Stop! I am a Chippewa, but I cannot eat my brother's people. My blood is in his arm, and his blood is in my arm. I cannot eat my own blood."

"But we can eat all the English."

"Give me this knife. I believed you were false Chippewas, and so I came back."

"Let go the knife!"

"I will not let it go. I have brought a present to give in exchange for my brother. You taunt me with going hunting. I went to my lodge."

"Yes; Wawatam goes to his lodge in time of war."

"It is well for you now that you hold the knife. I am no woman, but neither am I the eater of my brother's flesh. Will the Chippewas take my present and let him go, or will they cut down one of their chiefs with their enemies?"

The Frenchman who held the light waited the end of this dispute with more visible anxiety than the Englishman. Henry began to feel that no Indian could kill him. His brother Wawatam seemed to prevail. The squad of warriors remembered their promise. They were a people ruled only by persuasive eloquence moving on the surface of their passions, and they felt in their own lives and practices the force of Wawatam's plea. The Chippewa in his grasp inquired where his present was. Wawatam said it was in the kitchen below. His antagonist relaxed hold, and Monsieur Langlade lifted the candle high to light the descent.

A knot of bodies emerged from the foot of the stairs, Wawatam keeping close to Henry. Rain was pouring down the kitchen windows in sheets, showing diamond lights against a background of blackness. The muddy prints of many moccasins tarnished Madame Langlade's scoured floor. Her husband's face was drawn with anxiety to have the business over and the party out of his house.

Wawatam dragged his packet from the spot where he had dropped it, and stooped to one knee while he uncorded it. Fine skins and wampum enough to satisfy the greedy eyes around him were displayed as well as the light could display them. Wawatam was quick in completing his tacit bargain. Only a few of his tribe were parties to the exchange, and so jealous and changeable is the savage nature that he could not count on their continued acceptance of it.

"Take your brother," said the man with whom he had struggled for the knife; and Wawatam at once opened the door and slipped with Henry into the storm. He gave no backward glance at Chippewas dividing the furs, or the Frenchman waiting their pleasure, but he and Henry made their way around the house and toward the palisade gate. It stood wide open. They could see the whiteness of the hissing lake. Wawatam spoke at his brother's ear, wind and water even . then half destroying the sound, and directed Henry to tread close behind him.

They stumbled across bodies. Lightning smote the world vivid with its glare, and Henry saw one of those faces; but Wawatam swept his eye around for living and drunken Chippewas. He mistook a shout for the outcry of discovery and pursuit, and leaped with Henry through the gate into deep wet sand.

The Chippewa chief pushed his canoe directly out, and bade his brother get in. They were off from the shore in a breath, each balancing himself and paddling with desperate care. No Indian would ordinarily trust his life to the lake on such a night. If driven to the water, he would skirt the shore. But Wawatam steered out across the straits as well as he could in the darkness. Their first efforts kept the two men from seeing anything but the lake heaving its awful shoulders to swamp them. They rode swells which made the little boat shiver. Foam hissed around them, and stuck upon their persons in white specks. But as their muscles grew to acting with automatic sweep and balance, the universe around them could be swiftly noticed. There was no sky except when the lightning spilled it. Then vision flashed abroad to immensity, and suddenly contracted to blindness. Thunder bellowed among the islands, and shook like some substance afloat in the air, until the long reverberations lost themselves. The fort was an opaque mass against a low-lying foreground, lighted in one or two spots. White Canadian houses behind it showed their sleek walls as phosphorescence, and then vanished. The scant forest on the mainland pricked out its pine points, and withdrew them again.

Rain trickled down Henry's face, and his long hair clung in tendrils around his neck and ears. He had no hat. Wawatam, who never wore anything on his shaven poll but a chief's decoration, shone when electrical light revealed him. Their peril grew as they advanced farther into the waste blackness. The Englishman answered the motions of his pilot with steady nerve. That day had given him sights which seared the mind. He was ready to drown, though if the canoe swamped he felt he might mechanically swim.

From the general direction of their zigzag tossing he guessed the port which Wawatam hoped to reach. But no talk could pass between the two men except at the top of their voices, and they kept silence.

Henry knew very little about this Chippewa who had adopted him with the superstitious selection peculiar to the Indian nature. Wawatam had begun a year before to make him presents, speeches, and lover-like visits. Henry had responded, amused and touched, giving presents in return, and practising his store of Chippewa words with a good will. He felt no sacred claim upon the Indian, and acknowledged in himself no necessity to risk life in such a service as this. The character of the silent red man loomed before him a colossal manito, of unsuspected worth. He had seen the brutal side of savage nature; he was seeing now its spiritual side.

The trader understood that Wawatam had a family, and he thought of the squaw waiting in anguish, and looking from her lodge at this black chaos. They had been out so long that he forgot every function of life except an automatic balance and the fight with the paddles, when he began to take notice of a roseate star in the north. Lightning blotted it, but in darkness it burned steadily, and he finally saw it was low against a mass of land.

"The island of Mackinac?" he shouted in Chippewa at Wawatam.

"Yes; the Great Turtle," shouted back Wawatam.

Henry had not crossed the straits since his arrival at Fort Michilimackinac, and the islands were unknown worlds to him. He was the pioneer of the English fur-trade, and had ventured with audacious courage to the wooden outpost poorly maintained by a mere advance-guard of his nation. Received coldly by the settled French, with warnings by the soldiers, and sullenly by the Indians, he had not plunged into the woods at all, though their spring freshness tempted him, and the glare on the sand was a monotonous sight, but remained about the fort, guarding his stores, and making such headway as he could into savage friendship. The Great Turtle, or Mackinac, Island, was about five miles distant from Fort Michilimackinac across the strait. On clear days, in the elastic and transparent air at the mouth of the lakes, he could see the white cliffs of Mackinac half smothered in foliage. He knew the Chippewas venerated it with superstitious feeling. They gathered there for their great ceremonies. It was sometimes thronged with lodges, and sometimes left in solitude. A colossal manito brooded over the place, and other invisible beings worked spells there. Henry smiled in the darkness at being flung for safety, through flood and storm, upon this enchanted land. Wawatam was attempting as well as he could to put his brother in barbarian sanctuary.

A smaller island lying south of the Great Turtle reached out for them with a long phosphorescent arm. Pale green and diamond lights flashed from this sandy bar as the water rolled over it, coruscating and changing through countless tones of color. Wawatam steered far from the uncanny grappling-hook. Henry was ignorant of these insular coast-lines. When, therefore, after long darkness the dying lightning made its revelations, he was startled by the nearness of the shore. It stood above him. The canoe tossed like a chip at the base of wooded heights. The low-lying star which he had watched emerged from the windings of their course a conflagration. They no longer needed the lightning. A fire roared in a stone fireplace on the beach, and rose-colored smoke escaped from the penthouse of its front. Logs of some size, and much small fuel, heaped the hearth. Henry could hear through the hiss of water a crackling of pine and cedar. The fireplace was in a sheltered cove partly walled around by rocks. On the beach floor and in front of the glare two figures moved about, the rain scarcely veiling them. Henry was so wet that he knew his fingers were shrunken and white around the paddles. The June night chill reached his bones. The fire, like a home hearth inviting him to this unknown coast, appealed with a power that his flesh instantly acknowledged. But the tenders of it so surprised him that his discomfort was forgotten in straining sight at them. They were two white children, a girl, and a short, grotesque boy. The girl stood well within the shelter of rocks, and directed the boy in his laying of the wood. Light poured upon her, now rising so that Henry could even note the flush of her cheek and the lines of her eyebrows, and now sinking until her face became a rosy blot in the dimness. She appeared to be dressed in gray gull-feathers lying smoothly downward, untarnished by the rain.

This plumage gave roundness to her young shape. Her hair hung in two large braids down the front of her shoulders. When the boy had put wood on the fire, he resumed turning a leather string on which a piece of meat hung roasting. The string was fastened to a crosspiece upheld by two forks set in sand and stones. At a corner of the hearth a bark platter of fish stood ready, savory incense suggesting itself in the air above. Henry noted all these things with a quick glance or two; the picture of the wilderness kitchen so illuminated filled his mind by a single impression.

Such a narrow strip of beach paved it that every swell of the lake threatened to overwhelm the fire. Yet the high-riding water always broke hissing among fragments of rock lying scattered at the edge—waste stuff that it had carved out in past ages when it made the fireplace. Not a spatter of foam reached the girl or the supper she was tending.

She and her companion watched the outer darkness, but, dazzled by the light in which they stood, they were blind to the speck riding so near them. Wawatam knew every inch of the Mackinac coast; but remembering all they had dared that night, Henry thought he was absurdly cautious about landing his canoe. He held it out in the weather, and moved on eastward, until the kitchen's shine lay behind them, a heaving bar across the water. They passed a turn of the cliff, and after much skilful paddling came into a softly rounded cove which could scarcely be called a bay, but which sheltered and let them easily on shore. Henry guessed at these things by the massing or retreating of glooms above him, and the line of the water. The organ breathing of evergreens overhead convinced him that pine and cedar clothed these heights like a garment.

To feel hard pebbles underfoot, and to grasp a rock or a bough, was returning to life after long suspension in what was neither life nor death. They pulled their canoe in, and Henry helped Wawatam conceal it and the paddles in a thicket of balsam fir which scratched their hands with its wet needles.

Their path under the cliff was a very narrow one. Several times they had to wade, and the lake washed their legs as they hugged the wall. Wawatam led the way.

He grunted cautious words to Henry when the Englishman fell behind in crossing a pool or lost the direction among rocks. Again they saw the shine on the water, and felt it reaching to them through chinks of the trees. Wawatam suddenly raised his voice in a low, penetrating hoot. He held the trader in a pause. A similar call answered him from the kitchen.

They came to the broadening of the beach and the roaring fireplace. If it had seemed cheerful from the lake, it seemed home's own altar now, and the offerings smoked in readiness for two hungry, exhausted men. Henry looked eagerly around. No human being was there; not a rustle came from the shadows. He felt disappointed. He felt even tricked by the influences of the island. Two figures had certainly passed before the hearth. In this empty place he had traced the outlines of a girl's eyebrows. No noise of climbing, no crackle of broken brush, betrayed a retreat. There was only the crackle of the fire, and to that he was obliged to give himself, turning himself in luxury and drying his steaming clothes.

Wawatam seemed only half pleased by what the vanished islanders had done for them. He took his knife and swiftly cut small pines, piling them between the glowing fireplace and the lake. It required so many to make a screen high enough, that Henry was quite dry when Wawatam finished his task.

Still looking waterward with misgivings, he made his English brother sit against the pile, hid from possible voyagers, while they ate their supper.

Before Wawatam sat down he brought water from a spring near by. Listening, Henry could distinguish its gush from the falling of the rain. It came down the cliff, as he learned for himself later, but at that time he thought its small noise was simply an escape into the lake. The water and the venison and fish were delicious enchanted drink and food. Henry felt his blood revived with sudden impetus such as wine gives. It flew through his arteries, a distinct rapture. His eyes laughed, and the long taciturnity of the night passed away, like a trance. He wanted to raise a shout, and make his voice ring against the cliff, but the precautions of Wawatam were a warning to recklessness. So he only talked rapidly, managing the

Chippewa words as well as he could, but exuberantly slipping into English or French where expression failed him.

Wawatam listened, and answered seriously, or with a smile slightly loosening the corners of his mouth. He was glad his brother was safe and full of spirits. He was a straight-featured Indian, spare but sinewy. His face, as it dried in the firelight, showed a clearness of tint and a benignity unusual in his tribe. The draggling rain robbed him of no dignified effect in his clothes. He was well dressed in buckskins, the fringed collar opening and showing a clean-cut neck finely done in human bronze. Exposure to sun and weather had printed small radiating lines at the corners of his unshaded eyes. He was very little older than Henry, but his forefathers of the wilderness had left their somber and aging impress on him, as Saxon and Norman had left their brighter impress on the Englishman.

"My brother has brought me to a good lodge."

"Best not stay here long," said Wawatam.

"Have you some hole to put me in on the island?"

"A good hole," said Wawatam.

"You are not going to let your brother down like Joseph into some pit?"

"Joseph is not in a pit. Joseph stands on the altar," remarked Wawatam, whose knowledge of Hebrew history was bounded by the mission church at L'Arbre Croche.

"I did n't mean the saint. But I shall be safe wherever you put me."

"There is no pit," said Wawatam, "except the rift; and that is not a pit. It is where the heart of the island broke."

"What broke its heart?"

"Once the manito left Mackinac: that broke the island's heart?"

"Did he ever come back?"

"Who could stay away?"

"Is your lodge on the island, Wawatam?"

"Yes."

"You are never afraid of the spirits?"

Wawatam glanced around under the rims of his eyelashes. He did not answer, but excused the light inquiry of his brother.

The young Englishman rested against his evergreen cushion and looked at the mysterious cliffs. He was open to beautiful impressions. Strong love of the wilderness had brought him to this perilous frontier. Before penetrating a yard into the island he felt its influence like the premonition of love. It drew him and claimed him. The fire gave him a flickering sight of crumbly limestone full of little sockets and cleavages filled with moss. Gnarly pine-trees hung down, distorted with gripping the rock. Wet young ferns breathed somewhere under cover, their shy maid's breath being brought to him by the dampness.

"Who were those spirits tending the fire before we landed?" inquired Henry.

Wawatam relaxed his mouth-corners more, and answered: "They were no spirits. They were part of my family."

"But seen from the lake they looked like a white boy and girl."

"Yes; they are white."

"How did you get a white family, Wawatam?"

"Not all my family are white. My old grandmother is Chippewa."

"How many are there in my brother Wawatam's family?"

"Three: my old grandmother and the boy and girl."

"Was their mother a white woman?"

"Yes; both their mothers were white."

"Then they are not your children?"

"No; the boy is my adopted son. He has but one eye. The girl is my wife."

Henry had a sensation of discomfort marring his perfect physical happiness. As he lowered his eyes to the glowing coals he asked himself why an Indian like Wawatam should not have a white wife if he wanted one.

"Your wife?" repeated the trader.

"She will be my wife," corrected Wawatam. "She lives yet in the lodge with my grandmother. When peace comes I will take her in my canoe to the priest at L'Arbre Croche. No time for marrying now. Too much war; too many evil birds making a noise."

"Who is she, Wawatam?"

"She is a girl without father or mother."

"I understand, then, that my brother has at some time kept her from being killed as he has just kept me from being killed. Is she English?"

"No; French."

"But your people are the friends of the French."

"I did not say I had kept her from being killed."

"And is the boy her brother?"

"No; he is English. He is what you call an idiot," said Wawatam, with unconscious humor. "But we do not call it so." Henry laughed.

"The English at Michilimackinac certainly behaved like idiots to-day when they threw the fortress gates open. And nearly all of us have died the death of idiots. My escape was by no wisdom of mine."

"No more time to talk," said Wawatam, rising. "You must hide."

He took the largest firebrands and plunged them into the lake. The logs and coals he put out with water carried in the gourd which had supplied them from the spring. A hissing white vapor and clouds of ashes drove Henry up from the evergreens, and darkness grew where the hospitable hearth had shone.

As the ashes settled, and steam ceased rising, Wawatam spoke in the darkness to his adopted brother.

"I must go back to my tribe, to the feasts and war-councils, or they may search you out and kill you yet. They think I am only halfhearted in this war. The French girl that is to be my wife will have to bring you food, for there is no one else on the island but my old grandmother, and the boy, who could not remember."

Henry drew in his breath with a quick impulse. But he waited with all the gravity which this hint imposed. After a few minutes he made the promise:

"She shall be my sister as Wawatam is my brother."

The Indian on his side kept silence in the darkness. When he spoke he said:

"I will trust my brother."

He began the march, and Henry followed him. They took the same way along the beach by which they had come, wading pools and walking around rocks. The rain thinned, and the lightning had become a flicker on the horizon, but the angry lake still rolled in white ridges, and made a wide-spread noise of its wash on the shore. When they came to the cove where the canoe lay hidden, Wawatam waited and listened. Satisfied by sound or lack of sound which could not be detected by his white brother, he then made rapid progress. The ground stooped to them; the wooded heights sloped down to draw a lovely semi-circle, rounding the froth and glitter of waters. Wawatam did not follow the shore-line here, but struck up a long shoulder of hill, tracing some course he knew well, though the pine boughs had to be parted out of their way. Henry trod directly behind him. A hint of morning was already abroad, in that thinning of the darkness which is more the wan failure of night than the decided approach of day. Birds were inquiring of one another in their unseen retreats. Uncanny wings went past Henry's face, giving him a shuddering start.

"Bats," observed Wawatam.

Moisture in the evergreens and low, broad-leaved oaks rained upon them; but in all this indistinctness and blind following of his leader, Henry felt the exhilaration of the island. The wet was a sprinkling of balm. Heavenly incense from thousands of primeval censers filled the woods, and filled his spirit. Two or three times he thought he heard twigs breaking behind them, and told Wawatam. The chief listened with him once, and moved on undisturbed.

They had groped over many levels, through many mazes of juniper and hemlock and acres of thick-studded trees, when Wawatam ascended a little mound of flinty waste, and stood breasting a large rock covered with tangle.

"Here it is."

"What is it?" inquired the trader.

"The Skull Rock."

"Do we stop here?"

"You must creep in."

He pressed his hands on his brother's shoulders, and made Henry stoop to the low opening.

"Creep in as far as you can," said Wawatam.

"Is it a cave?"

"Yes."

"A large one?"

"Not very large. But you can hide there."

"Will my brother rest in this cave, too?"

"No; the storm is past now. I must go back to Michilimackinac before the sun is up. It will be better if I am there in the morning. My tribe will not know how far I have brought you."

"But you have had no sleep all night."

"No matter."

"And the lake is still covered with whitecaps."

"The paddling will be easier when there is some light."

"How soon shall I see my brother Wawatam again?"

"Not soon, unless there is danger. My brother must lie quiet and wait in patience until I can find some chance to send him to his people."

Henry squeezed the Chippewa's hand. This was no farewell for Wawatam, who took his white brother in his arms. The forest breathed around them, and bits of sky above the trees were translucent with rising light.

"Bless you, old fellow! I am not worth half the trouble you have taken for me. I hope I can do something for you some time, and that you 'll never regret you saved my scalp."

"Good-by, my English brother."

"Good-by, my Chippewa brother."

Henry crawled into the cave's mouth. The dank odor repelled him, and he turned his head back to ask Wawatam, who yet stooped watching him:

"No snakes in here, I suppose?"

"No; Skull Rock is a sacred cave. No snakes on the island except two kinds, and they have no poison."

The trader crept down the cavern's slope. He looked back once more to see the red face at the opening of the rock; but Wawatam's moccasins were silently moving away on their journey to Michilimackinac.

The place was paved with uneven fragments, which rolled under Henry's hand as he groped. It was an irregular hollow, turning at right angles in the rock, and when he reached the turn he thrust his feet backward into the further mystery, and stretched himself out with his face to the opening. He was stiff from his long paddling, and faint from living such a day. The elixir of the island no longer reached him. The presence and restraint of a stoic like Wawatam being taken away, he gave himself up to weakness, and slept like a dead man, unmoving and pale.

PART II

THE GHOST-FLOWER

"SING again, George."

"George has sung."

"I say sing again."

"All good."

George sang again, if a nasal droning broken by barks and bird-trillings could be called singing. The singer had doubtless learned his music in the school of the Chippewas. Henry heard it in the cavern underneath, and knew what figures were sitting on the top of the rock among gnarled pines and tangled growths.

"That will do, George. That ought to wake the Englishman if he is ever going to wake. I am tired of sending you down to look at him."

"Pretty man in the cave," observed George.

"The English all look well enough, but they are a bad people. I do not like them."

"Not like George?" remonstrated her companion, with a whine. "George all English boy."

"You great baby, can you not be sure I like you when I am making you a pair of new moccasins? You belong to the island. But the English — they are quite another sort; though I am glad I learned their language in the convent, since you can never speak French."

The sweet contralto voice, using his mother-tongue with an accentuation which he had often called "frog-eater's brogue," and using it to denounce his nation, made Henry smile in the cave. He was in need of amusement. As he tried to move himself on the uneasy lumps of his rock mattress, a shudder ran through him. Daylight penetrated far enough into the cavern to show him that he was lying on human skulls. Bald, narrow frontal bones and eyeless sockets stared through the drift of old leaves. Henry crawled over these specter faces toward the entrance. There he found a roasted bird and some venison on a birch dish.

His movement was heard by the two overhead, and they scrambled off the rock. The girl's voice hissed a low warning. "Monsieur must not come out of this cave until he is permitted."

Henry stopped, and the boy, tearing through bushes, appeared in front of him as a guard. He rolled his head at Henry, and enforced the uttered mandate by adding, "All good."

The look of eternal infancy on his idiot face was most touching by daylight. Stunted to a grotesque broadness and knottiness of figure, he moved like a little bear on its hind feet, and his dress bore out the resemblance. It was all in one piece, a bifurcated apron made of a dark blanket, which fastened at the back, and was drawn by a cord around the neck. His eyebrows and hair were of a sandy tint, and his skin maintained a raw pinkness. His single eye had the penetrating stare, and probably the microscopic power, of a bird's.

Henry leaned forward, and looked around the edge of the cave for the white islander. She stood hidden among the trees, but promptly repeated:

"Monsieur must not come out."

"But, mademoiselle, there are skulls in this rock."

"They are nothing but the heads of good Indians. Does monsieur find them very bald?"

"Quite so, mademoiselle."

"Monsieur's skull will soon be as bald as they are if he ventures out before it is safe. The chief commanded that he should lie still."

"When did you see Wawatam?"

"About dawn he met us as he turned back to Michilimackinac."

"You came up from the beach behind us, then?"

"Yes, monsieur. Eat your supper and be quiet."

"My supper? Is it evening?"

"Nearly evening. The light yet slants through the woods."

"Thank you, mademoiselle, for your care of me."

"It is nothing."

"But I heard you say you were tired of waiting for me to wake."

"Because the chief said you must be told to stay in the cave. George and I have waited since noon to tell you."

"I will obey every word you say," promised Henry. "May I add to the trouble I am giving you, and ask for some water?"

"George has been three times for water, but we threw it out as it grew tepid. Go again, George, and fill the gourd, and bring it quickly."

"Thank you, George," said the trader.

"All good," responded George. He ambled away, in what direction Henry did not notice. Hungry as the Englishman was, he did not begin to eat, but looked at his hands and weather-stained clothes. The instincts of civilization were stronger in him because he thought the white islander yet stood at the cave corner. Her appendage, the boy, was long on his errand. Henry could hear the rustling noises of the woods. He spoke again, having waited in vain for her to speak.

"Have you lived on this island a great while, mademoiselle?"

She did not answer. Henry looked cautiously out, though he knew he could not see her. Having given her message, and sent George for the fresh supply of water, she had gone her own way. When George at length handed in the gourd, he looked uneasily

WAWATAM.

around instead of at the man who took it. He struck off through the woods as true as a dog on the trail, and Henry ate and drank, hid the food which was left, and crept back among the bones. He thought of himself with contempt, skulking in a hole and giving a woman the care and labor of feeding him. To act and to dare were natural to him, rather than to burrow and to wait.

He lay a long time thinking what he could do for himself. His goods were confiscated. Supplies which were on the way from Detroit to him would probably be seized, also, and his various clerks robbed as they returned from trading in the interior. There was literally no help for him except in the friendship of Wawatam. His only relative in America, Sir William Johnson, was too far away to know of the fort's loss soon, except by guessing it from commotions among the Indians eastward; and his friend, Monsieur Cadotte, at Sault Ste. Marie, might be unable to keep the Lake Superior tribes from rising.

Henry regretted dropping Pani's blanket in the attic. When he dropped it he expected to leave his body also. There had been no urgent need of it until he tried to make a bed in the cave. He had slept well on bones before he knew they were there; but as darkness filled the woods, and pressed their company on him, the pulses of his body made them creep and palpitate under him. Yet he forced himself to lie still in the unendurable place, until a human shape darkened the entrance, whispering to him.

"What is the matter?" inquired the startled Englishman.

"Come with us instantly, monsieur, and be as silent as you can."

Glad that it was necessary to change his place of concealment, he obeyed. His moving hand touched the remnants of his supper.

"Shall I bring the gourd and dish with me? They may be found here."

"Bring them? Yes. George will hide them."

Putting the things past herself, the French girl drew Henry by the arm. He stood up outside the cave, stretching the cramp from his joints. The bushes were shaking where George disappeared. It was not a dark night like the stormy one which followed the massacre, but a white one, lacing the ground with every little twig. The moon in her first quarter already rode high. This dense island forest was a world of magic. Henry felt its spell as he followed between walls of foliage. There must have been a path, but to him it was a submerged struggle through leaves. His guide parted the way easily, as a fish goes; a shorter and broader body had passed through before her. The trader did not know who might be following behind. He reveled in this swimming of the wilderness. He had capacities for woodcraft. It gave freedom to a repressed and manly part of him, and in the darkness of the buried path he breathed largely. Sweet pine, bruised by hurried treading, gave out a tea-like fragrance. The rank, loamy breath of moss, that night prayer of wooded lands, made itself stronger than any sensation of danger. Sometimes through a break in the foliage he could see spacious chambers of the woods hung with hemlock tapestry, to which the moon wedged an entrance. A man must cut his way to such a spot, and Henry thought one of them might be his destination. But the French girl led him out of the tangle, and he saw through a great arch of stone the clear surface of the lake. It startled his pulses to come out of the New World's heart facing this old ruin, the water-carven mimicry of a gigantic castle gate.

His leader took him again by the wrist, and drew him away from the stone arch and down into the growths on the cliff. A path descended toward the lake, so narrow that one person had barely foot-room, but partly hedged by trees and bushes along its outer edge. To miss footing here was to tumble into unmeasured depths. Henry followed, steadying himself by a hand on trees, or by clutching roots and the stone ribs of the island. This thread of a path went down to a slab of rock which glaciers had cut out and canopied for a seat. George was already resting in a corner of the niche in the bluff side, and the other two sat down beside him, and waited in silence for what was to happen. The girl leaned forward, watching the path.

The lake's irregular rush upon its beach could be heard below, and a thousand cries of little living things which make populous the wilderness sounded far and near. No crackle or stealthy swish of steps overhead could be detected.

Henry contrasted the figure at his left hand and the English boy at his right, the high intelligence and the gentle brute, dependent on each other for companionship. It was a satisfaction to sit beside the woman. She whom he was to let alone had unusual influence upon him. None of the rawness of girlhood appeared in her face. She was his mother for the time, taking care of him. The trader noticed her dress. It was not the plumage which he thought he had seen in the beach kitchen, but a garment of dark-brown wool, made of a blanket, like George's pinafore. A cap of birch bark, having a rosette of curly fibers, was tied over her hair.

The twig and leaf tracery in front of them was as black as ebony against the silver air above the lake. All the world glistened with dew, though their shelter was dry. There was a rift in the trees towering up from the beach through which they could see the moon's track on the water, spread broadly with cloth of gold.

"Is that your brudder?" George inquired, leaning forward, and touching the French girl to make her look at him. He turned his thumb back at Henry.

"Yes," answered Henry; "I am her brother. I promised Wawatam to treat her as my sister."

"All good," said George.

"What is her name, George?"

"My name is Marie Paul," she herself answered, relaxing from her vigilance over the path. She looked at the Englishman. He was distinct enough in that filtered light, and she thought him the best-made man she had ever seen.

"George and I saw a strange canoe in the bay," she explained, guarding the pitch of her voice.

"Perhaps Wawatam has come back," said Henry.

"We know his canoe."

"Did you see who was in it?"

"There was one person paddling, but it was not Wawatam."

"I might have taken my chances with one Indian."

"Not while you slept. The Skull Rock may be known to all the Chippewas; but this place is known only to George and me. We made the path to it."

Henry's heart swelled because she had brought him to a place known only to George and her.

"Then even Wawatam knows nothing about this cave?"

"No," said Marie.

"Why did you go to the bay in the night?"

"To watch it."

"But you were up watching last night."

"One does n't mind that here on the island."

"Have you lived on the island long?"

"It is two years," answered Marie; "for I was past fifteen the first time I confessed to the priest at L'Arbre Croche."

"Was the priest at L'Arbre Croche willing for you to live here among Chippewas? Why does n't he send you back to your own people?"

"How can he, monsieur, when my family are all dead?"

"Then you have no relatives?"

"Nobody but the old Indian woman that I call grandmother."

The French predilection for Indians made Henry smile. "Would n't you rather live among whites?"

"Monsieur, I could not live away from this island. When you have been here awhile you will understand. It bewitches you. There can be no place like it. The chief took us one winter to St. Ignace, because there was once the missionary village, and we could be warmer. I watched the island by night and day across the ice. Its white breast was my mother's breast. In the spring I was thin, and my eyes were hollow with longing for it. You cannot live away from the island, monsieur, when it has once taken hold of you."

"You are happy?"

"Everything is happy. What is there to make one miserable? George and I have found the place for your lodge, monsieur."

"I can stay here," said Henry.

"No, monsieur; this will not do: you must have a lookout as well as a hiding-place. To-morrow, if that canoe is gone, the grandmother will give us mats, and you shall come and help us build it."

"I shall be glad to," said Henry. His large eyes were watching her with interest.

"You are not like the other English I have seen," observed Marie. "You have gentle manners. It is beautiful in a man to be gentle and obedient."

"The English do not generally obey the French," said Henry, smiling.

"No; they love to drive us, to seize what is ours. I have heard it said that is why the

English have just been killed at Fort Michilimackinac."

"Who was there on the island to say that?"

"It was the Chippewa grandmother."

"I will not drive the French, nor seize what is theirs," promised Henry.

She laughed, showing white teeth. The trader wondered how a girl nurtured by the Chippewa grandmother could keep an exquisite person.

"You must stay here the rest of the night, and until we come for you."

"I will."

George was asleep in his corner, and as Marie passed in front to wake him, the trader turned himself to the same task.

"You must be very careful; he might make a noise."

In her anxiety she barred Henry back. The touch of her firm, healthy hand tingled through him.

"All good," said George, when stood upon his feet and warned to be quiet. He took hold of Marie's wool frock for the ascent.

Henry also stood, and drew aside some bushes which were in their way. His other hand went out solicitous to help her, but was withdrawn with a self-restraint which she keenly admired.

"I suppose you won't let me go up to the top of the cliff with you?"

"No; stay here. It is after midnight. Good morning, monsieur."

"Good morning, mademoiselle."

SUNRISE brought a perfect day. So transparent was the dazzling air that from the bay one could see distinctly strips of meadow and woods and the white French houses on the mainland, and bars of sand edging the water there. A narrow pink cloud floating in that part of the sky made the lake blush in a long line under it. On the high ridge of the island were open, sun-flecked woods, inhabited by white birches with broad, gray girdles around their waists; and scattered around their feet lay the parchments they had dropped. Henry climbed these slopes as wilfully as a truant, Marie guarding his horizon, and George traveling sturdily at his heels. They had two loads of mats to carry to his lodge site, as well as his provisions. These goods waited under the bushes while they all loitered. The suspension of peril causes a greater rebound than its removal.

Great blossoms of pink and yellow fungus spotted the ground. Their fleshy beauty was dry to the hand, and, broken, they showed sound hearts. Daisies and blush-colored bell-shaped flowers were thick in grassy stretches; and the maples were uncrumpling their very last web leaves of unripened red. The evergreens were full of small brown-crimson cones like luxuriant bloom, and perfect top tassels snapped thumb and finger at the sky. In the open woods ancient beds of leaves had been beaten down to mold, forming a neutral-tinted background on which delicate etchings of foliage were traced by the sun. Henry looked around this lucent green world, feeling that he could never forget it — its transparent shadows, the scattered light upon the ground. They followed a deer-path up the ridge, which Marie said was the usual trail to the lodges.

"Because the strange canoe is gone, we must not think there is no danger at all," she repeated.

Henry smiled at care for his life, or his goods, or his future. The present was to him the prime moment of existence. All his days had led up to this one, the beginning of some golden period unknown to men who lived in anxiety and toil.

"The island has bewitched me," he said.

"I knew it would," she answered, looking him through with clear gray eyes, glad that he was made to own its influence. She was always handling the material of life with joy and wonder.

A distant gleam in the woods, unseen by any one else, startled her from the path. She ran over the quaking and rustling forest pavement, and dropped upon her knees.

"Ghost-flower," observed George, halting, and he brought his face about for the concentration of his eye on the distant object. He followed her, tumbling at full length once, and striking the leaf-dust from himself when he arose.

Marie beckoned to the new inhabitant of the island. She was sure there could be no rapture like the first finding of Indian-pipes. Her breath paused on her lips as she pushed dead leaves aside and showed the bunch. Their glistening white stems, on which the lucent scales were as delicate as gauze, stood in a family perhaps fifty strong, closely and affectionately holding their waxen heads together. Through some of them flushed a faint pink, but the majority palpitated with a spirit of lustrous whiteness in every part, strangely purified from color.

"Look at them," said Marie, impressively. "They are my own flower."

Henry knelt down and looked at them. He looked also at her face in its birch cap, her wide brows, the rounded chin and beautiful throat, and the braids hanging down over the swell of her young breasts. She lifted her eyelids, and shared the great pleasure of the Indian-pipes with him.

"You may take these. But as soon as you touch them they will begin to change. Does n't it seem impossible they can turn black?"

"Do they turn black?"

"Quite black, if they are handled. But left in the woods, they go away like spirits."

Henry did not touch them. If he had not been there, she would have sat a long time by the ghost-flowers, watching the glistening wonder of their open cups. She broke off a handful of them, and gave them to him as a queen confers an order. The trader said within himself that he did n't know what to do with the things, but he readily cumbered one hand with them. Marie then took some for herself, and looked George over to see if he were fit to hold any. The poor fellow began to settle in his clothes, and to seek the pockets which a white boy has a right to find in his trousers, but which Marie would not sew into his since he tore them out with agates and quartz. She had herself tied his drawing-string, but her practised eye caught his neglected points, and she put the flowers behind her.

"George will have to go to the lake and wash before he can have some. We must all turn back before it grows any later. Monsieur's lodge is to build. Monsieur," inquired Marie, "what are you called?"

The trader answered that his name was Alexander Henry. She heard it without approval.

"That may do for Fort Michilimackinac, and other parts of the world, but here you are Félix and Amédée. In the morning you will be Félix, and in the afternoon you will be Amédée."

The Englishman accepted this French christening with a flush of satisfaction. "Why not Amédée in the morning, and Félix in the afternoon?"

"I do not know, except that it is the other way."

They moved back through the light woods over delicate traceries of foliage shadow, and scrambled down a steep part of the ridge, holding by mossy hummocks to keep from falling, and came to the bushes where the mats were concealed. Henry and George took the loads, and Marie led on the path she wished them to follow. There was no marked footway, but a parting of the forest led them into a large open space from which could be seen the high plateau of the island. Morning lodge-smoke ascended in blue, expanding streamers from Wawatam's hidden camp. Marie knew the old grandmother was trotting about those upper woods, engaged in the slave work of an Indian woman.

Pale-green juniper spread its ropy branches on the ground in every direction, but she piloted her stumbling carriers through the thinner snares. Then they entered once more that world of pines and cedars which guarded the coast, and were long making their way among boughs, though the ground here was as smooth and clean as hard clay to the foot. Everlasting twilight checked the little growths of the woods, and pine-needles made an aromatic soil of their own.

Henry's blond face was flushed with the tramp and portage when he pushed through a tangle of vines and young oaks to where Marie finally waited. George ambled close behind, enjoying the world and his usual occupation. It was nothing for George to tramp the length and breadth of the island, only to fish or find agates at certain points. His one eye saw the happy side of life. Had he watched the massacre at Michilimackinac, it must have typified to him some bliss bestowed on the victims. He would have said, "All good."

"This is the place, is it not, George?" asked Marie.

They looked down into an amphitheater padded with moss and curtained from the lake by bushes. It was really one amphitheater over another, irregularly broken with cushioned ledges and hidden rocks. Little trees were massed together around it. A smell of loam as sweet as roses came up from the place. George focused his eye, and nodded.

"I was sure of it," said Marie, "though we never came through the woods before. Our canoe is hid on the beach down there. You cannot see this cove from the beach. It is surprising that we ever parted the bushes and found it. I see the rock for your table, and the tree for your tent-pole."

This world of velvet greenness was different from anything Henry had seen. It was a cascade of moss forever in the act of falling down a mountain-side. The distant horizon could be traced, bounding the lake. Far off the blue water shaded to grass-green stripes betwixt zones of purple. He had a speechless feeling that he was in the hand of some mighty spirit that changed Nature and him from moment to moment.

"Where are we?" he inquired.

"On the eastern side of the island, beyond that arch of stone that you saw in the night."

"Then we cannot see the mainland from here?"

"No; but you can watch the strait."

They let themselves from rock to rock into the lower amphitheater, and laid down their loads. George and Henry cut poles. They varied his dwelling little from the common Chippewa lodge of conical shape, with rain-proof mats bound about it for shingles. The forenoon was spent when it was done, and its door-flap curled back, showing the snug interior. Marie had it closed around the top because its occupant would dare build no fire within. He did not know how far she searched for arm-loads of sweet pine to make him a mattress. They all worked at overlapping and fastening the mats. The flat rock she called his table stood near his tent entrance. Marie lifted from the cove side a fleece of branched moss which nearly covered her, and spread it over his table. Dry, fragrant bits stuck to her wool gown. Her eyes were happy. She had never felt before in such harmony with all things. You could scarcely hear the water lap the beach. There was no intrusion of sound as it rippled.

But a pair of eyes which were not happy came stealthily to a rocky buttress, where they could watch as from an upper window the beautiful court below. Their dark and piteous brooding lasted out the afternoon.

Many of the Indian-pipes had come to

camp headless, the slim decapitated necks reproaching their bearers. Marie brought wet sand from the lake, and made a mound for the surviving ones to stand in beside the head of Henry's green couch. She took George to the water's edge, and washed his reluctant face and hands. He whined; the fervor of her lodge-building had given him reason to hope she would forget his face and hands all day, and perhaps until the hour of driving him to that hated spot where she made him bathe.

"Now dry yourself in the sun," said Marie.

"Poor George!" complained the English boy. "Why brudder not wash too?"

"He is older than you," explained Marie. "He knows when to wash without being told."

"Poor George! Water so cold."

His closed eyelid had always a touching expression of trying to help his single eye plead with any persecutor, and Marie stroked him tenderly, picking bark and moss branches off his clothes.

"I will go with you to fill the gourd," she promised, and all his distressed creases instantly reversed themselves.

Henry came out with the gourd. The beach was made of round stones, which rolled under the foot, and turned walking into a toil if not a danger. The high sun beat upon Marie's cap, and her hair clung to her moist forehead, but she drove the Englishman back.

"Monsieur Amédée, you must not come out here."

"There is n't a canoe on the lake anywhere. No one can see me."

"I won't permit you to come out, Monsieur Amédée."

"She queen," said George, turning his thumb back at Marie. "Brudder better mind her; George does. Chief does, too."

Henry laughed, not at the undisputed autocrat, but at his own squawhood. His pliancy to her wishes was what most pleased Marie in the task she had undertaken. The tall leaning saplings laced themselves undisturbed betwixt him and the outer world. At first he sat down in the abundant moss, wishing for a good pipe of Indian tobacco; and then he thought of opening his provisions and spreading out the dinner. The earth was silent, for here he missed even the chirping of insects. It seemed so still one could hear a pine-needle fall; so still the soul's motion could be heard. The sweet, elastic air of the island filled him with vigor. He wondered that this waste of his vigor in a hidden depression of the cliff did not annoy him more.

Henry was on one knee arraying the vivid green tablecloth with his bark dishes, when a gathering rustle of the lake startled him. It was a hiss and a rush like the disturbance made by many canoes, though without the dip of paddles. He parted the bushes, and looked anxiously out. Often from Fort Michilimackinac he had seen white butterfly-wings of sails blowing across the water or making broken glimmers far off; but now not a thing could be discovered on the strait. The round island opposite, wooded to its edge except that spit of sand which stretched a grappling-hook westward, was by all tokens a deserted place. There was no perceptible change or increase of wind. Henry noticed, however, a roller forming in mid-channel, and sweeping as though tipped toward him. It broke hissing on the pebbles, and the little disturbance was over. Once more the lake was a sapphire pavement scarcely crinkled with iridescent spots. This commotion was merely its trick in the straits, beginning and ending without apparent cause.

When Henry had set the table, he climbed the broad track carpeted with ferns, which led up the amphitheater. Half-way up were three trees sheltering a natural chair of rock, amply carved, and high backed. He carried much dry, vivid-colored moss, and padded it, the drapery overflowing to a foot-rest below. Cups and little trees and branching tendrils of the moss were wonders of beauty. Henry enjoyed them as a barbaric embroidery which he could heap on Marie's chair. The rocky balcony was directly over him, and jealous eyes watched this preparation; watched his neglected golden beard and mustache and clustering hair, and the solicitude and sensitive motions of his fingers. Dirty buckskin would not have spoiled the Englishman's supple presence. His dress was substantial and rich, and, in spite of hard usage during his escape and hiding, it remained the dress of a gentleman.

Marie and George came to the broad, thin layer of waterfall which they sought; which ran first over a bed of moss, then threaded downward in inch-wide channels, dripped from rocky shelves upon a terrace, and found ways between rifted rocks to the lake. Dense woods stood above it. And here a sucking and gurgling of the water through pot-holes made Marie lift her hand and George wrinkle himself in apprehension. They both knew what this jerky and fantastic booming was; but she loved the superstition, and the boy frightened himself with it.

"Giant fairies!" whispered George.

"Yes; they'll catch us," said Marie, and he bellowed as she seized him to run.

Tribute being thus paid to the giant fairies, George straightway forgot them, pulled off his moccasins, and rolled up his trousers, to wade up the steep to the clear tap which he knew Marie preferred.

She held the brimming gourd while he sought a flat stone for a seat. One moccasin was tied when her outcry of discovery brought him erect.

"O George, you are almost sitting on gull's eggs."

Three pale-green eggs, spotted with brown, lay on the open beach. They both stooped down and handled the pretty things, holding them up to the sun.

"We will roast them," decided Marie, balancing the gourd. "Take this, George. It is I who will carry the eggs."

She packed them with leaves in the pouch hanging from her girdle, a brilliant piece of embroidery done in pink and yellow quills by the grandmother.

Henry heard the voices of his camp-makers approaching, and the crush of revolving pebbles, and the girl's scream. She was supporting herself on her hands when he ran to her, and George stood fixed, holding the gourd in a trustworthy grip. The boy was trying to see what distress on the lake made Marie weep, and drive to the canoe that very Englishman she had been so anxious to keep under cover. The Englishman found the boat, and flung it unhelped across the beach. A fish-hawk was dragging a robin through the water to drown it. Marie had seen the hawk drop like a stone with its prey, and she stumbled as she ran for the canoe. The fish-hawk, beaten off by the paddle, left the red-breasted bird, and soared away, indignant at killing prey for big unfeathered creatures, yet satisfied that its work was well done. The robin was past fluttering when Henry lifted it out of the water. It was drowned, and its neck was broken. He laid it in the canoe, feeling that this was a tragedy which grosser sights had robbed him of the power to mourn as he should.

And it was a delight to be floating upon liquid air. Sunshine lay on the bottom of the lake. Pebbles were glistening money. The shining bed rose deceitful to the very hand, until you dipped a paddle to touch it, and found it was fathoms below. That pale blue medium clarified these depths which dazzles us in the sun-warmed air overhead. Such transparent, sky-born water could be no kin to the frothy surge through which he had paddled for his life two nights before. When Henry drew the canoe on the beach, he saw that Marie was painfully trying to stand. He hurried with the robin in his hand, and put one arm around her to support her.

"I can walk," she declared, her face strained by the effort. "Run in, Monsieur Amédée, and leave me alone."

"You are hurt. I wish I had let the robin go. The fish-hawk drowned it before I could reach it, anyhow."

"Let me have the poor thing. O little

bird, how it pained me to see you dragged through the water!"

She stood on one foot, and held the robin against her shoulder, smoothing its wet dark feathers.

"You must let me help you," said Henry.

"I have only bruised my knee. A girl who lives with Chippewas does n't mind that. George has gone for leaves to put on it, and to-morrow it will be well."

Marie limped a step or two, and physical anguish whitened her lips. Without further parley Henry lifted her in his arms.

"O Monsieur Amédée, you will break the gull's eggs! We want to roast them for our dinner."

"Birds and eggs are nothing to me," said the Englishman.

He blamed the dead robin; but Marie held it and her pocket up, and guarded them from the boughs. He set her down in the lodge, and turned his back upon the little homestead, feeling disturbed as by a catastrophe in his family, until George ran whimpering in with some healing plant, and Marie finished her surgery. She looked out of the lodge when free to announce it, and called:

"The gull's eggs are safe."

"Now I breathe," mocked Henry. "I have kicked about a great deal of moss on account of the gull's eggs."

"Oh, but Monsieur Amédée," Marie laughed, "this is not a serious hurt, indeed. It will heal in a few days. You should have seen George's sprained foot. Father Jonois, the priest from L'Arbre Croche, had it in clay, and made him lie still for a week."

George stooped down and felt of both his feet. When he identified the one which had been sprained, he crumpled his face with an expression of great suffering, and offered it to Henry to look at.

"Give it rest, my son," responded Henry, paternally, and the boy sat down in literal obedience, and took it upon his knee until something else attracted his light attention.

Marie crept out of the lodge. The jealous eyes in the balcony saw her lifted again, laughing and startled, but confident in the gentle strength of her bearer, and put in the mossy chair. Her spirit came and went in her face, eagerly remembering mother-fond-lings and mother-care, and wistfully looking forward to some unrealized good. Her little ears, the shadings of her skin, and the soft rounding of her features tempted as a child's cheek tempts. The island shyness was in her withdrawal from Henry when he would have placed her more to his satisfaction in her chair. But this day, to which two had come from partial isolation in the wilderness, was more effectual than months of ordinary meeting and parting.

"We must now build the oven, George," directed Marie. So George brought pebbles from the beach, and he and Henry scraped a hollow in the moss and lined it with them. The dryest bits of wood from drift washed high, and bleached in the sun, were put into the hollow. George knew how to start a fire by the Indian method, but when the spark answered his efforts, and was sheltered with cedar boughs, both he and Henry were at much trouble to keep the fire clear so that little smoke would rise to betray the spot. Red coals were soon fading to ashes, and the eggs, wrapped in wet leaves, put under them. It was a long meal, as protracted as some culminating feast, and accompanied by guarded talk and laughter. Trivial things were no longer trivial; they had become intensified life. George, unconscious of his chaperonage, sat picking his egg-shell beside the table. But the Englishman sat near Marie's feet, and told her parts of his experience; concealing, as men do, some of it which direct-gazing eyes like hers might not look at. Yet he had the virginal innocence of young and beautiful manhood. This day hinted to him possible harmonies in the dumb instrument of life which he could not interpret. To make wealth had been his best understanding of living; to brave danger and exchange his youth for money. There might, however, be a perfection of existence for which there was no equivalent.

A young balsam-fir, small and tough, and as straight as a needle, grew near the table. Marie selected this for a staff, and Henry cut it down and peeled it, carefully removing the branches, which grew in circles around the stem.

"George and I will have to take the canoe," she said regretfully. "We brought it here for you; but the trail from the bay will be easier for me."

"Let me help you to the lodges," urged Henry.

"No; George will help me. The chief left word that you must not risk being seen about the lodges."

"When is Wawatam coming back?"

"I do not know. We will feed you with the best we have. George and I have a garden in the open land at the other side of the island. There may soon be vegetables for you. My salad was out from the ground last week, and I have a bed of little herbs."

Henry pictured the boy and girl working in their garden, and felt a homesick desire to follow them to the spot, and see again the plants which answer civilized culture.

"I wish I could dig."

"Perhaps you may if that strange canoe is really gone, and no other comes."

George gathered the fragments of blackened egg-shell and put them into the oven, and covered the pit of ashes with fir twigs. The day was nearly spent when he held the canoe to the beach and the other two came halting toward it, Marie looking abroad on the lakes and feeling the influence of late afternoon. Accustomed as she was to their changes and misty effects, they gave her beauty at this gazing which they had before withheld. She stood still between her staff and Henry, and loved them anew. The sun was already behind cliffs, but not swallowed by the water. His warning was bringing stray island birds home. The evening colors were not yet created; only a fore-glow hinted what they might be when sunset was complete.

The Englishman owned no hat to take off, but he raised his hand to uncover his head as the boat moved away. He and the French girl both smiled, and she admonished him afresh, so he went back through the curtain into the loneliness of his little world. The day spent in the Skull Rock seemed an experience at the beginning of life. He felt sure Wawatam could not send him to Detroit. Savage living meant irregular meals and wild diet, and animal wariness in going about; yet he wondered if he would be domesticated at the lodges when Wawatam came back, and if they should pass the winter on the island.

His camp was becoming a pit of gloom, and he thought of putting his provisions in the lodge where he could keep them from small night prowlers. He found rolled up in the pack a deerskin bag holding an entire set of dressing-tools which he had once given his brother Wawatam, who hung them up unused. The joy of a civilized man in brushes overbalanced all Henry's losses. He stood with the bag in his hand, blessing the fraternal impulse which had made him attempt to groom his brother, when the top of the green amphitheater populated itself to his dilating sight. Pani, the Indian girl who had concealed him in Langlade's attic, stood up from creeping on her hands and knees. She had appeared as silently in the time of Henry's peril at the fort, and he glanced sharply in every direction, his blood leaping at that peculiar swell and gush of the lake which he knew must be only a ripple.

Pani stepped as deftly as a cat down the irregular slope, keeping her eyes on the ground she trod. Nor did she look up when the Englishman met her, asking in haste:

"Are the Chippewas coming, Pani?"

The Indian girl shook her head. Her arms hung humbly by her sides.

"Do you bring news from Michilimackinac?"

She again shook her head.

"Did you come here by yourself?"

Pani nodded. The toe of her right moccasin worked back and forth in the moss.

"Then it was your canoe they saw in the bay. And you paddled over alone from the mainland? That's not an easy task, and you took many risks. What made you do such a thing?"

She lifted her eyes, and gave him a look which confused his speech. He felt ashamed that his strongest conscious desire was to have this squaw, who saved his scalp, back in Fort Michilimackinac.

"I have wished for your blanket, Pani,—the one I dropped in the attic,—more than once since I came to the island."

"I brought it," spoke Pani in imperfect French.

"You are a good girl. But I don't need it now. Wawatam's family have built me a lodge, and made me very comfortable."

Henry noticed the bronze of her arms in their trinkets of whiter metal, and the coarse, strong threads of her hair. The language of her attitude embarrassed him. He swung the deerskin sack in an uncertain hand, and turned partly away from her, wondering what he should do. Pani spoke again, and the guttural fact which she uttered made him color.

"The ghost-flower girl, Wawatam's."

"I understand all that, Pani," said the Englishman. "Sit down, will you? You must be tired." No heart could feel more gratitude than his felt; but the droll dismay of a man who unexpectedly finds himself too attractive appeared in his face; and Marie saw it.

The wash of her returning canoe he had taken for the ripple. Henry understood why the white children came back in such haste and silence. Behind Marie's face was George's. Her lips were parted to give warning.

She was not conscious of spying on the other woman, but studied Pani's errand intently, leaning her head sidewise to get a better view betwixt the bushes. This barbaric figure, though coming from the settlement, bore the stamp of the wilderness; as Marie, though inhabiting a wild island, had still the undescribed air of the women of France. The difference between them was more than a difference of race; it was a difference of spirit. But the white girl took no thought of herself in contrast with this new comer. The cruel amusement of youth appeared in her eyes and at the corners of her mouth. She resented vaguely as in her own person the drooping humility of the Indian girl.

Henry exclaimed with too much eagerness when he met her eye:

"Mademoiselle, Pani has come over from the fort. This is Pani, the only friend I had when the garrison was killed. She hid me in Langlade's attic."

"Does she bring word that any Chippewas are coming?" inquired Marie.

"No; she knows of none."

"Did the chief send her with any message?"

"Did he, Pani?" said the Englishman, passing the inquiry on. But the reticent envoy made no reply.

"I am afraid she has been about the island hungry since yesterday, for it must have been her canoe you saw."

"That is true, monsieur, for we have just found it again."

"Can't you take her to the lodges with you?" asked Henry, feeling his brain emit the proposition in a flash.

"Certainly," answered Marie, with sincere readiness. "The grandmother will make her very welcome."

"Go, then, with mademoiselle, Pani. It was good of you to remember me, and come so far to see if I were safe."

"Let us go, Pani," said the French girl's persuasive contralto. "The sun is setting. It will soon be dark in the woods."

Pani gave her a slighting glance. The southern Indian's shape rose, the shoulders drawing backward and the aboriginal features rearing themselves; and turning her head toward Henry, she scorned his tame care with the bitterest look he ever encountered.

The three Europeans watched her supple back as she mounted the ascent of rocks and ferns. Even George dumbly felt her hurt, and would have restrained her. His one eye remained focused on the pines which closed after Pani until Marie pulled him to the canoe. Reluctantly handling his paddle, he sent the boat out on a pink sheen, reflecting sunset. Rose-colored air softened near cliffs and distant islands. Eastward there was no horizon line, but a concave hemisphere with little parallel lines of pink vapor drawn across it. A triangular ripple was broken in the motionless lake by the canoe. Already the arch of rock with its avalanche of waste below was a savage ruin, framing darkness.

Henry called once after the boat, but got no reply. He thought of the night woods and an Indian's skulking; and then he felt ashamed of himself for imagining that a gentle and merciful creature like Pani could do harm to any other woman.

He sat down in the lodge door, his aimless hand encountering the drowned robin, which Marie had left there. He took it up and stroked the wet feathers, for its little plumes still lay penciled close against its breast; and while he stroked it, his own breast rose and fell with the strong sigh of a man who suffers unconfessed pain.

PART III

THE RIFT IN THE ISLAND

ASHES as soft as down and as fine as the motes which swim unseen in the air blew from a pine fire toward the lodges. There were two of these conical houses, standing near together and facing the west. The space of fairly level grassy land was surrounded by oaks and beeches, which arose in strength, stretching their limbs abroad and making shady arcades all around it.

Marie Paul sat on a bench in one of these shadows, her quill-work in her lap, watching the Indian grandmother drag fuel up from the forest. In times past she had put herself heartily to such tasks when George was not at hand, sparing the aged back which bent to so much labor. But now her gaze at the old woman saw nothing; it was indifferent to the outer signs of life. Her languid head rested against the tree behind her; lace-work of the pine-ashes formed upon her knee without being distorted by a movement. She was conscious of a stifling breath or two as the blue veil was curled around her by the wind. This was the second day Marie had crept to the bench that her Latin prejudices long before caused to be built in the camp. As for Wawatam and his grandmother, they preferred a mat on the ground, and George sat anywhere, with adaptability unusual in his race. But Marie must have a raised seat in the shadow of jutting trees.

She listened for George's return. She had trusted him twice with the Englishman's food. The first day George did not find Henry in his camp, and she sent the boy back in the afternoon. Henry had then returned from tramping through the woods.

"Brudder lonesome," declared George. "Brudder can't keep still."

The squaw pushed her fagot under the pot, and squatted on the windward side of the fire. Her coarse hair hung down her back. A toothless smile opened the puckers in her face as she met the girl's eye. Marie wondered if her own neck would ever fall into such leather creases, and the underlying bloom fade and blacken in her skin. A week ago she had looked forward to age as some indifferent change to which she must come with rocks and trees, expecting dignity from hoariness; but now she dreaded the remote robber with unaccountable terror. It was a wicked thing to value her tinted, supple flesh with such passion; Father Jonois would lay penance on her if he discovered this state of mind.

"Noko," spoke Marie, using the familiar abbreviation for grandmother, "are you very old?"

The Chippewa woman turned her head from side to side mournfully—the universal sign-language of barbarian women when expression fails them. "Old as the summer-maker, my child."

Marie no longer cared eagerly for the summer-maker and his kindred myths.

"Do you like to be old?"

"It cannot be helped. You bear children, you draw wood and dress meat, and the seasons pass. It cannot be helped."

The fate of aboriginal woman stared Marie in the face. Her black lashes made narrow lines of her gray eyes as she pondered the sight. By some way she arrived at the inquiry:

"Noko, what is your opinion of men?"

"They are all the same, on island or mainland, my child. When you are beautiful they kill one another for you; when you are ugly they sneer at you. Two chiefs once fought over me." The squaw laid her arms on her knees and laughed in them at the recollection.

"But white men—they are not like red men."

"Yes; all the same. Men are men. The more they come soft, humble, creeping the ground like the panther, the more they will eat you up and laugh at you."

"Then, Noko, why did the good God make women to believe in them?"

"Because the good God knows they can't get along without women."

"But there must be some good men, very high above panthers and such things. Is your own grandson a panther?"

"No; my grandson he is a good man," answered Noko, with tribal jealousy. "Much better than the French or English."

"I should like to ask the priest about it;

but there are some things I cannot ask him, no matter how they perplex me. We ought to be old first, Noko, and when we have wisdom enough, grow young."

"Would n't do," said the grandmother, rising to stir the pot. "Never would marry any man at all, then."

The savage cast of her copper face, with its prominent nose-arch and cheek-bones, was not repellent. Since coming to the island Marie had made the best of Noko's company. It was scarcely improving; she went to the woods and the saints for society; but it was comforting. The primitive woman is a human hen; such wings as she has are spread to shelter her brood. Noko cooked choice bits for the growing girl, and on summer evenings often sat chanting for her the folk-songs and stories of the Chippewas. Noko's knotted red hands were spared many a hard task by skilful younger ones. The grim but wholesome old heart had indeed but one fondness in its age, and that was not for Wawatam. The grandmother was only proud of him.

A phœbe-bird darted calling across the open space, its speck of shadow moving like a flash. Some comer startled it from the lower boughs. Marie turned her head, and saw the extended body of a deer rising up the slope, and George's face under it. Henry and Wawatam were behind him, coming to the lodges together.

Wawatam called in Chippewa to Noko, who answered him; and George threw the deer down before her. The chief turned toward Marie. From a stalking, stalwart Indian he changed suddenly to an apologetic figure in dejected buckskins. She had climbed upon the bench, and held to the tree for support. Her back was toward him and the Englishman. Every soft curve of waist and shoulder was followed by the close gown; half-curls powdered her neck in a short, raveled plume, the hair parting above them in a white track from nape to crown. Immature as it was, this girlish figure had enthralling force which made it a central presence.

Henry did not understand why she hid her face. His voice had a piercing appeal as he asked:

"What is the matter, mademoiselle?"

"The chief knows," answered Marie. "Ask him."

"War-kettles boiling at the fort," explained Wawatam in guarded Chippewa to his brother. He put his hand on his mouth. To have the hated feast detected the moment of his return was confusing.

"His face looks like a wolf's," said Marie.

"But I did not want to taste it," pleaded the enforced cannibal. He cast a glance of wrath at his grandmother, who had revealed that such feasts were held after every Indian victory. It was very unpleasant to have women meddle in tribal politics. Noko and George were in consultation about the deer.

"Consider what a poor lot we were at Michilimackinac, mademoiselle," said Henry, recklessly. "If Wawatam has eaten a bite of the garrison to save the trader, he has afflicted himself to little purpose, and is to be pitied."

Wawatam's eyes were uneasy, and his usual placid benevolence was driven out of his countenance. He knew that Father Jonois would exact penance from him as a Christian Indian; but what was a Chippewa chief to do when his people boiled the English and made him dip his hand in the kettle as a test of good faith?

Marie's trifling with his dignity was the amusement of his life. When she was a year younger she had beaten his shoulders with a balsam stick for presuming to slight some command of hers, and Wawatam had doubled himself over and taken this squaw-drubbing with silent delight. Yet she depended on him as a father, and spoke of him as the chief, never using his name in the careless English fashion. The relations between the Christianized savage and his French foster-child were so natural and guileless that in all her imaginings she had never pictured Wawatam as her lover. There was in her blood no instinct against him except the instinct of rating him with George simply as one of her good creatures. Wawatam knew how to fight, how to hunt, and how to manage his fraction of the Chippewas. He could command any unmarried squaw of the tribe to his lodge. And he had thought it would be easy, when the convenient time came, to mention to Marie that they would take the sacrament of marriage together at L'Arbre Croche. Father Jonois did not discourage this plan.

"Tell him to go away," said Marie.

Wawatam did not understand her English. In camp his entire family spoke Chippewa. He turned for interpretation to Henry, the wrinkles at his eye-corners drawn down by a sinister look. Henry felt it was a climax in his experience when he was forced to mediate between an elected bride and a cannibal husband from whom she hid her face. He had seen her moving like a bird through the wilderness, a part of it and its free life. Disgust for all the conditions which hamper existence here filled him with sudden desire for death. He wondered at his hiding and his pains to prolong such contemptible misery.

"She says she wants you to go away."

Wawatam spoke angrily to Marie in Chippewa:

"Why must I go away? Is it because the Pani woman has been here and brought me a message?"

"Do you mean the Pani woman who came to monsieur's camp? She did not take a message. And if I had sent you one, would you have heeded it any more than you did the priest, who must be at Michilimackinac now?"

The abjectness of a smitten conscience returned upon Wawatam. He said in gutturals under his breath, "The Pani woman was a fool!"

"I am a very bad man," he acknowledged, taking Henry into new confidence with twinkles of the eye.

"You are so bad that I cannot endure to look at you. You are so bad I am afraid no saint will intercede for you. Go into the woods and fast."

"But if the chief begins a fast now he will leave his brother in danger."

"Why did you bring him here if there is danger?"

"My brother is safest where I am."

"But why have you come?"

"The best trail leads past the lodges."

"What is the danger?"

"A band of warriors have come from Detroit. He is the only Englishman left. They told me they must have him."

There was silence in camp. George lolled on the ground at a distance, watching the grandmother's skilful knife as she skinned the deer. The sun was warm on his back, and his hair showed glints like gold-stone. He would never be lashed by the mysterious tides of his own spirit.

"What are you going to do?" asked Marie. She had not yet turned her face from the tree.

"Going to put him in a canoe to go to Sault Ste. Marie."

"When?"

"Now."

"Does the chief go with him?"

"No; it is in Madame Cadotte's boat that he will go."

"Where is it now?"

"Coming from Michilimackinac to take him off on the west side of the island."

Marie knew without explanation that this would be the safest place for Henry to embark. There was a sandy, level beach where the water was deep enough to allow the approach of even a sailing vessel, which could then move on unobserved around the northern shore toward the Sault. She had once seen Madame Cadotte, the Indian wife of the Frenchman who was called chief of all the Indians around the Sault.

Rapid Chippewa questions and answers escaped Henry, anxious as he was to understand them.

"But if other canoes meet them, will he not be seen?"

"No matter," answered Wawatam; "he is a Canadian now, like the Canadians that row for Madame Cadotte."

Marie half turned herself and looked at Henry. He was so changed that she wondered how she had been sure of his presence when he and Wawatam were ascending the slope together. Some of his own garments were discarded, and he wore in their place the blanket coat of ordinary Canadians, and like them had a handkerchief knotted around his head. His face was clean shaven, and it gave her through every revealed line, and through fixed eyes, the silent passion and longing which had already grown mighty under repression. That chemistry of the spirit which draws two irresistibly together, through space, through obstacles, through time,— which may work anguish to both, but must work because they exist,— kept these young creatures an instant conscious of nothing but each other. Marie resisted it. She sometimes had such intimations of happiness when lying in the woods with her head beside a bunch of Indian-pipes, or when a height was hooded with thunder-clouds while the beaches flashed in the sun. The joy was like a recollection of heaven; blessedness came near; you could not account for it. She thought it had come oftener when she was a child. But her capacity for it grew. Every atom of her body glowed with intense life. She hid her face against the tree.

Wawatam's features hardened. Any man but his English brother might have died for such a look. His natural hatred of Anglo-Saxon stock urged him to feel for the scalp-lock on that golden head. But he was bound by visions and traditions stronger in his spirit than the Christian religion to keep in safety the man of his adoption. He said to himself in Chippewa, "It is the chief and not the Pani woman that was a fool."

"Come on," he said curtly to Henry.

The trader, conscious of the offense he had given, yet drew a long, reluctant breath.

"Good-by, mademoiselle."

"Good-by, Monsieur Félix."

"Heavens! *Félix!*" Henry drew another deep breath.

"It will not be Amédée until afternoon."

"In the afternoon I shall be far from the island."

"Poor Monsieur Félix!"

"Thank you, mademoiselle, for your thousand kindnesses to me. I blame myself for the hurt you got on the beach."

"What a tender conscience you have, monsieur!" She was no longer his careful mother, but a mocking creature, giving him one laughing look over her shoulder. "It was the fish-hawk."

"I hope your lameness is cured."

"The only thing that hurts me now, monsieur, is that the chief killed gulls to make my feather dress, instead of fish-hawks."

"Then you have a dress of gull-feathers?"

"Yes; it turns rain."

"You wore it by the fireplace on the beach the night I came to the island?"

"Yes, monsieur. The chief was a long time collecting breasts. And when he brought them to me I cried — that so many birds should die to cover me. If I but had a cap to match it now," added Marie, drolly.

"The French have tender hearts," mocked Henry.

"It is true, Monsieur Félix. They never desire the death of any one. It is not necessary for them to recite from their prayer-books as the English do, when the priest says, 'Thou shalt do no murder'—'Lord, have mercy upon us, and incline our hearts to keep this law.'"

She mimicked the congregational chant, and Henry laughed aloud. Wawatam was in the tense attitude of his forefathers watching an enemy from ambush. When her voice mocked and Henry laughed the chief's face relaxed. He picked up Marie's quill-work from the ground, and, before laying it beside her, passed his fingers along the shining stitches, as one might try some chord which would not vibrate. Living two years under the thumb of a French islander had bred softer practices in him than he cared to have his braves see.

"I wish I could do some service for you, mademoiselle," said Henry.

They were parting forever. And why should they not part forever who had seen each other less than a brief week? Lakes, and land, and perils, time and silence, would crowd between them. The summer day was perfect around them, the sun turning shadows black on a vividly lighted earth.

"Good-by, mademoiselle," repeated Henry.

"Good-by, Monsieur Félix," she answered, keeping her back to him.

"Will you give me your hand?"

Marie extended a hand behind her.

"That is the left one."

She gave him the other, and it lay unresponsive in his while he wrung it.

"Are you angry with me?"

"Oh, no, Monsieur Félix."

"I have missed you these two days. I'm very glad I found you on the island," blundered the man. "It has been a pleasure; I hope you will be happy."

"No more time," said Wawatam.

Henry kissed the round and childish hand. He was permitted by the usage of the times to do that. Wawatam had seen officers at the fort kiss Madame Cadotte's hand, for she was a woman greatly respected. Marie felt the touch of lips. She let her hand fall as he turned away, and stood still with her face toward the tree.

Bushes stirred as Henry and Wawatam brushed through them on the direct trail to the western landing. Wawatam bade George, as he passed that happy boy, go back through the woods and watch for Indians from the fort.

"What do with them?"

"Nothing. Bring word back to the lodges."

Reluctant to leave the deer, George's backward looks dwelt with it, and not with the men. But Noko lifted herself from the quartering, and watched the Englishman out of sight. The trees soon received him, and she was not sorry. He had a handsome white face, and eyes which looked through you with an influence like the moon. Marie had relieved her old bones from tramping to his haunts with his food, and she hoped her grandson was now taking him off for a long hunt. The less one saw even of adopted Englishmen the better.

"Watch Indians," said George, making a half circuit of the bench to face Marie, and intimating that he waited for his usual companionship.

Marie gave him a smile of the lips, and picked bark from the tree, letting it fall on fungus that spread a pink umbrella between the oak's roots: many bits glanced off, but one balanced itself and resisted efforts to displace it.

"Chief says watch Indians," repeated George.

"Bring my stick and cap from the lodge," said Marie.

George brought them, and stood like a young bear on his hind feet while she let herself down from the bench. He would have dropped on all fours and made himself a stepping-stone, had any other mind given him the impetus. The two went down the trail toward the beach. As soon as they were below the level of the grandmother's vision, Marie paused in her limp, and said:

"You watch the bay while I watch the woods."

George's face fell into creases of distress. "George all alone," he complained. "George all alone twice."

"But I cannot run with you now. I am a hundred years old, like Noko."

George still squirmed, his red face having the blank yet wrathful expression of a wilful baby's.

"Very good. Take me with you then. But you must carry me," said Marie.

George had carried her up from the bay the night of her accident. He remembered the strain, their long rests, Marie's vain efforts to help herself, and his exhaustion when they reached the lodges. His loose and fleshy body had not the muscular compactness of Wawatam's or the mature strength of Henry's. He yielded, and went on alone with his rolling gait, looking back as long as he could see her.

Marie turned around the base of the camp, and put her halting limb to reckless use. She knew short cuts among the pines, and ventured many before untried. She flung herself through mats of juniper in the open places as a Highlandman crosses streams. In times past Marie had loved to test her endurance by long journeys afoot, and labors about the camp. It was sweet to work to the point of exhaustion, and then throw herself on her bed of hemlock and blankets, and sleep as the rocks sleep. Her vitality was so full that every awakening from sleep became a new birth. She ran out as rosy as Aurora under the morning sky, her flesh tingling with the delight of being alive. But this haste she was making to cross the island had none of the laughter of youth in it. The regular sweep of the muscles which becomes a silent music, and makes of walking a graceful and glorious function, was lost to her as she panted along. Last week a goddess moved from beach to headland as freely as the light; to-day a limping girl, pallid with the effort, tried to reach the north shore before Madame Cadotte's boat should pass by. She had no reason for wishing to see Madame Cadotte's boat; but when one has sat still awhile, it becomes impossible for one to sit still any longer.

The high land sloped gradually to alluvial stretches in the direction which Henry and Wawatam had taken, but Marie climbed directly down a hillside so steep that she was obliged to hold to trees and the knotty earth itself. She missed her hold, and slid dangerously, but the scratching and bruising did not detain her an instant. Near the bottom she noticed that her balsam staff was no longer in her hand. It was not worth the hard ascent, yet she climbed back in panting haste, and found it lodged in a bunch of fern. A stout stick could have been broken below with half the pains.

The sun stood overhead as she hurried through the lower forest. Her course was as nearly straight as the eye could direct it, and she came to the lake in time to see a boat with sails set getting beyond the eastern shore of the island. Flecks of red like the kerchief-bound heads of Canadians glimmered against the white. No other visible thing moved on Lake Huron.

It might not be Madame Cadotte's boat. Marie sat on the rocks, watching eastward and westward until she lost it, and nothing else appeared on the void. A wind which she had not noticed in her rapid journey made indigo stripes across the water. There was a low roar as of little falls. Though white-fringed rollers ran before the wind, some clouds made flat, moving islands of their shadows. Overhead the light dazzled.

Moving from rock to rock, Marie waited along the beach. Jaded, and dragging her limb, she came to a remembered bluff. Some impulse of the wild things among which she had lived drove her to a hole under the bluff. It was necessary to descend among fragments of rock, and to stoop down to find it. She carried with her such moss as offered, and crept through a tunnel which led her into a high cavern. Water trickled from above through the place. She made herself a divan of the moss in the driest spot, lying recklessly at length, her head on her arm, hidden from the light of day.

The life of the woods and the hissing of the lake were shut out. Her consciousness extended only as far as the water trickling down her cell. Scarcely a glimmer of light came through the tunnel, for its mouth was sunk below the beach. Marie turned once in the afternoon, and changed the arm on which she lay. Time's divisions were lost; she had come upon the eternal now. Yet so much is the spirit in the body's keeping that her stupor passed to sleep, and she lay in that sweet death until forced to a numb resurrection. "Nothing matters," said Marie when she roused.

The lake was a sea of glass and fire, and the hush of summer night was already in the woods. The Detroit Indians might have crossed from Michilimackinac and scattered themselves in search over the island. Dew dampened her hair and the soles of her moccasins. The rapid fluttering of scarcely seen bats grazed her cheek. She kept repeating with dull conviction, "Nothing matters now."

Wawatam was not at the lodges when this limping figure arrived about moonrise. Noko and George were squatted in amiable silence by the kettle, watching a fragrant yellow fire lick its sides. Odors of venison and herbs came to Marie's nostrils. She had not eaten since morning, and, creeping to the outdoor hearth, she sat down with her family, laying her staff beside her.

This was the hour when Noko told Chippewa legends; but she did not speak a word. Some older story-teller was busy with Marie. George waited only for his supper. When Marie sat down in the night camp she never had the degraded feeling of herding with barbarians. These good creatures were her household. She often dipped out the mess for Noko, and restrained George's animal greediness. Clean birch platters were kept in readiness, and she had for herself a knife and spoon which Wawatam bought at the fort. The others preferred to use their fingers. To-night the grandmother filled Marie's bowl from the general dish and brought her knife and spoon. George was left to gulp unrestrained except when Noko hit him on the back to keep him from choking. Marie sat and looked at the fire, where beautiful embers crumbled, and ate her food without tasting it. The moon was white and large. It threw shadows of the Indian woman and George, and the dish between them, and a fainter shadow of Marie, across the smoldering log.

Those usual inmates of northern lodges, the silent dogs, were lacking in Wawatam's camp. None of them were running about the island, on account of Marie's abhorrence. They were not like the bluff, loud-mouthed mastiffs with which French children played, but uncanny, wolfish things, never seeking a caress, and springing voiceless out of thickets. Wawatam kept his dogs in another camp. They could find their wild living in the woods, whether led by a master or their instincts.

Marie crept into her lodge and dropped its flap. She took off her blanket gown, and put on another in which she slept, and combed and freshly plaited her hair. She had a pillow on her bed, a thing Noko despised. It was made, though, only of the dried needles of sweet pine sewn into a piece of coarse linen. Beside the high mattress was spread a skin on which she stood. Noko's bed was at the opposite arc of the lodge. No moonlight came through the mats, but a glimmer from the hole at the top rested on her head. Marie took her crucifix, which hung from a rib in the sloping wall, and lay down in her bed, holding it, and uttering no prayer but the dumb one of misery. She watched the poles intersecting the fragment of dark blue sky at the top of the lodge, tilting her head back on its pillow. Her knee felt stiff.

"This must be what the priest calls immortality," whispered Marie. "You cannot die."

She turned on her hard mattress, and resolved: "I will bathe in the lake early, while the water is cold. That will drive this strange feeling away."

She heard Wawatam in the camp, giving a string of fish to his grandmother. He had been out all the afternoon in his canoe. His returning without Indian followers was a dull satisfaction to her. Yet when a whiter pallor than the moon's showed between the lodge-poles, she put on her moccasins in haste to escape from camp, took her clothes and the thick linen towel which was kept for her use alone, and limped off toward the natural arch of rock. The dewy tents still swam in uncertain darkness. The sweet-scented earth gave back the old joy of morning to Marie. Crumpled mist arose, floating, and letting itself be wound slowly aloft. There was a steep descent to the lake underneath the stone arch, where a long avalanche had once fallen. Marie let herself down this rough stair to her bath. The limpid expanse of water increased the light. She could see as far as the well-known trees in front of Henry's deserted camp; but she turned her back on that place, and stripped for the plunge. Nothing was abroad to see her but the morning star. Her feet shuddered in the shallow water. She waded out and knelt, throwing herself forward and turning with a splash. The blue drippings of a glacier could be no colder. Streaming from crown to heel, her body the color of a rose, she ran behind a rock covered with pine shrubs, and polished her flesh to marble firmness. It was a delight to feel the blood palpitate against her very garments when she was clothed, and to climb the height like a giantess. The bruise on her knee felt this revival.

"Nothing ails me," exulted Marie aloud to the stirring birds; "I can plunge where Indian women dare not."

A family of mushrooms, their white, fleshy umbrellas half furled, waited beside her path, and she gathered every one. They would have to be skinned and salted, and soaked all day; but by night they could be wrapped in deer-meat with a husk of clay over that, and put under the coals to gather all the venison's juices. She was proud to feel an interest in the food-supply of the camp. "But if I had found them when monsieur was here," said Marie; and she stood still, her face changing.

The camp-fire lifted its delicate blue shaft straight to the zenith. George was helping Noko broil fish on some stones, and a bowl of sagamité was set out for the morning meal.

Wawatam had put on his best dress. The beaver robe which he wore only at councils was gathered around him and thrown over one arm like a Roman toga, showing the feather-work of his leggings and the rich embroidery of his tunic. He paraded himself across the plateau as Marie entered the camp, though through all his dignity the childlike savage betrayed a gauntness and anxiety of visage. She busied herself with the mushrooms. The amenities of civilized life he never imitated; but Marie usually said good day to him, and he stopped beside her aggressively. Wawatam despised mushrooms as food for men. The red lines in his face expressed disdain of such employment as he said:

"Put on your best dress."

Marie was startled.

"Do you hold a council on the island?"

"No. Go to L'Arbre Croche."

"I do not want to go to L'Arbre Croche to-day. It was only last month that I went to confession."

"Father Jonois will marry you."

"Father Jonois marry me? He cannot."

"He will."

"But no priest can be a husband."

"Myself," said Wawatam, slapping his breast; "I am the husband."

Marie threw her braids behind her shoulders, and restrained him by a sidewise turn of the eye.

"I will not go to L'Arbre Croche with the chief."

Her barbaric guardian did not know what abhorrence maids lavish on undesired suitors. In one instant he changed from her friend on whom she depended, and to whom she deferred, into a detestable pursuer. More than that, he robbed her of what he was before; and there was no other man on earth to take care of her. Wawatam, like the wolf-boy, saw his new shape himself, and he accused her in a guttural snarl.

"You would go with my English brother to L'Arbre Croche. You would be wife to him."

"I would not!" Her whole body flashed at Wawatam. "I would not be a wife at all. And you who have neither fasted nor prayed since eating man's flesh — do you think that Father Jonois would give the sacrament of marriage to you?"

Frontier priests were obliged to make the conditions of religion as easy as they dared for their wild flock; but he knew she was right. Father Jonois would not give him the sacrament of marriage until he had done penance for that sin detested in the committing. It was very hard to be a Chippewa chief and a baptized Christian, the brother, more

"BUT NO PRIEST CAN BE A HUSBAND."

over, of an adopted Englishman, when that Englishman was doubtless his supplanter.

Wawatam said nothing more, and after his breakfast went into his lodge. At the untrammeled Chippewa breakfast the chief sat on a mat outside his family circle. When Marie was hanging the blankets of her lodge to air, she saw him in his hunting-buckskins going down toward the bay. The subdued determination of his stride denoted that he was seeking his spiritual counselor.

George hesitated between Marie and the chief, his dull mind apprehending some change in his playmate, as well as an altered temper in Wawatam. He followed his adopted father at a distance, hoping to share the voyage to L'Arbre Croche, yet loath to give up his daily haunts on the island. Wawatam saw him and beckoned to him. The weak one of the household, making this dumb plea for companionship, was a comfort under the circumstances.

Marie brought wood for the grandmother. When Noko had no heavy labor she sat cross-legged on a mat, busying herself with the needlework of Indian women. Sometimes she trudged to the edge of the island, digging roots in the woods. Usually, however, she spent her leisure soaking in the sunlight while she sang in a monotonous whine, with the rising and falling abruptness of barbaric music, the songs of the Chippewas. When one touched Noko from without she responded shrewdly; but she knew the dignity of reticence and solitude. Marie was not afraid of being questioned by her.

When enough sticks were accumulated near the log which made their chimney-back, Marie went farther into the woods. Early morning was gone when she stood beside the rift in the island, though here it was twilight at noon. A drift of aged leaves had blown from the north for many a winter, and partly filled this crack in the island's surface. Its scar extended as far as the eye could follow, and its moss-clothed sides went mysteriously down into earth's darkness. Marie once descended within the gap, and caught her foot in an angle of the rocks below. Such gigantic lips in the ground's face were a strange spectacle. They threatened to yawn and snap a curious gazer in.

Marie walked along the verge to a place narrow enough for her to leap across. Not far beyond the rift stood a white birch like a marble temple. Its central pillar was massive, and delicate arches spread a drapery of foliage far and wide. There was not such another birch-tree on the island. The high ground on which it stood fell abruptly to a hollow at one side. Marie descended into this little valley, and knelt before the vision under the roots of the tree: a cavern of rock tufted with fern and velvet lichen; the most beautiful grotto that ever enshrined an image. It struck the sight like a miracle. The mighty birch flourished overhead, its bank of turf roofing this glittering cell. Nor was the image lacking. It stood on a shelf of the rock, a small plaster Virgin, which had been given to her by the priest for her chapel in the wilderness. Marie's last offering, some withered flowers in a basket of scented grass, stood on the cavern floor. The pitiful image, weather-stained by its western exposure, lost its immobility and swam before her eyes as she remembered the roving child who put that basket there. Her own hands, clasped upon her beads, were strange and far-away members—the hands of a girl that lived last week without any knowledge of pain, and vanished.

Her features took a wan tint from the dimness of that holy place, and her mouth trembled at beginning a personal invocation.

"O Mother of God, take this feeling away from me. Why has it come upon me? I have tried to be a good girl. Here is my dear staff, that I lay down as an offering to thee. Ever-blessed, I have such sinful love for this staff that I slept with it laid across my breast."

Marie covered her face with both hands, the rosary dangling from her fingers, and leaned forward until her braided hair lay upon the ground. "I will say that he is a heretic, he is a heretic, he is a heretic—but, O Mother Immaculate, he is the gentlest man I ever saw in my life! I shall never see him again—but give him to me—" she threw herself backward, breaking through mediation, and tearing at heaven itself with uplifted hands and a cry as strong as the throes of birth, "O God, give him to me—you must—I shall die!"

The tiny image on the shelf, the rustling birch, and the woods around her, were gone, and she was in infinite space wrestling with the master passion of the world, and learning that invisible things only are of account in this life. The human instinct of hiding passion kept her terrible weeping silent. And presently, exhausted by this prayer of anguish, and daring to look no more at the immaculate image, she fled limping from her chapel and lay down beside the rift.

On the opposite bank of the chasm a phœbe-bird alighted, turning its head inquisitively and considering her limp figure. It took its joy on the island untouched by any human anguish.

"I used to be like that," thought Marie, as the bird darted away. She felt deserted by companions, who found her no longer of their kind.

Her denial of love, her panting journeys, and manual labor to get rid of it, were ended as soon as that prayer to Almighty God burst from her soul. He knew what had happened to her. The saints and her mother knew. There was no use fighting it any longer. She was to live or die by this unconquerable force. Once Marie had wanted to be a saint, but now she greedily desired to be a happy woman. And this was a strange thing: that one should come, and look, and possess. She had seen officers from the fort in their scarlet coats without giving them a second glance. They were objects on a landscape.

Marie stared across the rift as if her eyes could penetrate woods and water-mists to the Sault. That light which falls on the spot where one's beloved stands, leaving the rest of the world in twilight, and hallows his country, giving it the sanctity of a shrine, now rested there. She did not know the world had come to her until it went away. To be where he was seemed the only good. With rapture she saw again the hopeless passion in Henry's eyes when he left her.

"You are mine," whispered Marie through space to the secret ear of that other soul who must harken. Her hands and feet were cold, her muscles were knotted, her face was white with the stress of this secret cry, "Come back to me! You must come back. My life is gone out of me. There is something the matter with the island. It has changed. You are the island to me now."

She let her face slip over the edge of the rift, where cool, dark moss could send up its breath to her, and the rock give her palpitating temple a reminding touch. The woods calmed her, their grays and greens and interlacing density of stems, and their whisper of a secret which has lasted from the foundation of the world, replacing her fever with a kind of beatitude. Power to project herself into the future was gone. Love is itself eternity. She took no interest in what might happen. The one fact of the universe was present with her. That primal instinct of young creatures to believe in and make a religion of the human being they love is one of the best and saddest traits of humanity.

A chill grew in the air. Marie felt it, but she no longer resisted the warfare made against us by inanimate things.

"Why did I hide myself from him the last day he spent on the island?" she asked herself, finding no answer. "And why did I laugh at that poor Pani woman? It is her turn to laugh at me now. But I would rather die by fire than let it be seen in my face."

Days and months must pass, and a message for which she could not help looking might never come from him. She would go to confession with concealment in her soul. "I cannot endure it," said Marie, sitting up in the darkening twilight. Then she remembered the chief's sudden proposal to marry her at L'Arbre Croche that morning. Father Jonois could forbid it; but who would teach her how to bear her invisible bereavement? She felt sorry for the chief with a tenderness which was not in her before she came to her knees at the tree.

A drop of rain fell on Marie's forehead. The white birch showed its marble limbs against gathering blackness. The east wind came on with a roar, bending little trees, and Marie knew that the lake looked as she had often seen it in a rainstorm, a dark yellow green, seeming to have sulphur in its depths; and that the sky above it descended in vertical strata, becoming one with it. In other times she would have run the intervening distance to see the lake during this disturbance, dashing out to a cliff, wet and bright-eyed.

The woods grew dark with a steady downpour, and on the churning strait zigzag tracks and curvings, such as currents leave on an ice-field, could be seen, changing as flaws of wind veered here and there. The air was raw; and when night came, autumn descended on the midsummer island. It was so chill that the eye suspected frozen spray upon the pebbles, and the white cliffs had a wintry look under beating rain. At midnight the blast was roaring against all the leaves in the uplands, and the pines tuned themselves to that high song they sing when the wind blows ice-laden from Labrador. It seemed impossible that summer could return, and incredible that she was there, huddling her million blooms, and cowering under this whip of the northeast. The change in the weather was a period set to life which had gone before it. Nothing could be again exactly as it had been before this chill came on the world. The icy breath was pure, but it blew the glamour off the island.

Nearly a week of squaw-winter crowded itself into the heart of June. All day a drizzle fell, and gray clouds dragged on the water, or tore themselves against headlands. The strait was a flume, hissing toward the head of Lake Michigan. Discomfited birds sat in shelter, calling sometimes to one another with a note like the cricket's. In the night the complaints of wild things could be heard.

Wawatam and George stayed at the fort, leaving the women of the camp to live on such food as had been accumulated. On the sixth day a slate-colored sky, cold and smooth, spread over the Great Turtle, unable to dull the new tints he had acquired. For the frost spirit had breathed fire, and hints of splendor appeared on masses of trees. Life warmed itself gradually, coming out of eclipse. Eastern islands, miles distant, showed their blue bars. In one place a boat's hull appeared, masts and sails lost in falling mist. In another a spot like a sun-dog shone on the water in the midst of opaque dullness, or it became a plate of copper moving across the lake. The clouds broke about sunset, and a mountain stood one third the height of the eastern sky. At the top a volcano of color burst out. The crater was a wide lap of fire. Rosy fog, changing its tints and pallors every minute, glorified all the northern world.

Across the iridescent pink water, and magnified by luminous air, came a procession of Indian canoes, avoiding the opposite sandspit, and beaching themselves in the bay. Always superstitious of life on the island, the ascending savages saw, though they said nothing to one another about, those brands of autumn color on a summer world. Noko's fire blazed, but she was somewhere in the woods, having felt the vigor of breaking up a winter camp revive within her after the east storm.

Marie sat alone in the lodge in her dress of gull-feathers. She had worn it during the wet days. Her braids hung over her bosom, touching the dejected face on each side, a fuzz of curling ends following their outlines with the distending effect of light. She was changed and deep-eyed. The winter week had ripened her. Marie had looked into that abyss of unaccomplished evil which sometimes appals saints in themselves. She who had laughed at the prayer against murder wished the chief would die. After prayers, and in her sleep, and at waking, that recurring potentiality still thrust itself into her mind—"Something may happen to the chief to-day." During the wet week there was nothing to do. She sat and moved the search-light of thought over her relations to the two men, Englishman and Chippewa. It was not hard for Marie to divine the chief's claiming her to Henry. She was Wawatam's squaw, whom gratitude forbade Henry ever to see again. She could appeal to Father Jonois; but the chief had fraternal claims upon her which must trouble her as long as he lived. It really seemed best that he should die. His dying would not bring her love back to her, but it would lift from her the responsibility for his unhappiness. Noko and George would be readily enough adopted by other members of the tribe. Then she could enter some sisterhood, and one of her penances would be for wishing that this very convenient thing would happen. Yet as often as it recurred to her she was full of terror at herself. The chief had made her the queen of his island world. No lonesomest and loftiest soul has kept itself from lapping edges with and being worked upon by the power or weakness of fleshly housed neighbors. Invisible lines mesh and restrain, or draw and distort, every one of us. The selfish and brutal break through, but fine and tender natures own the responsibility and endure the bondage as their part in the redemption of the world.

Once during the storm Marie had gone to the height above Henry's camp. She could not bring herself to descend into the amphitheater. The darkness of winter was lapped up in its glacial greenness. She saw her chair of rock; the wind had torn the moss cushions away, and heaped them on the place where he had sat at her feet. There was a story in the tribe of an Indian girl who had flung herself from a rock on the south cliff because her lover went away and never returned. Marie had laughed at that story. "I did not then know," she muttered, looking at the deserted lodge. Its mats dripped with slow, creeping rain. The seasons would pass over it, dropping it piecemeal. "I will never come here again," she gasped, and ran through the pine woods.

While this mysterious force worked in her she lay on her bed of nights in a waking trance, silent and nerveless, yet calling with compelling might to the man who had left her. The blood of her French ancestry—wine and fire which have sparkled and burned through centuries among the slower nations—made her swiftly a woman. She was the ghost-flower, sprung tall and lucent, a white flame of passion, in a night. "I would rather die because I cannot have him," thought Marie, "than never to have seen him at all."

The arriving multitude of Indians swarmed upon the plateau before Marie knew they were on the island. Strange warriors appeared among the Chippewas. The aboriginal visage, evasive and demon-like, was multiplied many times in the crowd. Totems unknown to her were tattooed on naked breasts and arms, while nearly all the dignitaries of the tribe stalked into view. Squaws carrying children on their backs, and having in their faces either the hopelessness of drudgery or the broad-cheeked look of honest beasts, defiled in silent rows behind their masters.

The hideous medicine-man was there, with moose-horns bound on his head, and his skin glistening with decorations as the moving body of a snake glistens. Marie looked away from him, and saw Wawatam coming to the lodges. She hid herself at the head of her bed, pulling one of her blanket gowns over her. He called to her in Chippewa, and also to his grandmother; but after stooping a moment at the lodge door, went away, evidently satisfied that the lodge was vacant. When Marie ventured to look out again, George crossed that triangle of the plateau which the opened flap described. He had the jocund leer of a tipsy faun, or any soulless animal made to take brandy in its food with astonishing and uplifting results. The pink of his skin was inflamed to higher color. Little hairs, long grown about his masculine chops, showed themselves with a new tendency to bristle. His hair stood in separate shocks. His pinafore trousers were greatly damaged, and it was evident that no one had driven George to water during the entire week.

"Father Jonois will hold the chief to account for this," thought Marie. She noticed the chief's changed look. Wawatam had been the most human convert of Father Jonois's flock. The cunning of barbarism was returning to his face. An unhappy Indian had not the resources of an unhappy European. Marie felt responsible for it. So mixed are our good and evil that she closed her eyes and made speechless appeal to heaven for the Chippewa she had been wishing dead. Wawatam was wary and expectant; he watched the borders of the camp. "He is afraid the priest will come and find him dealing with the medicine-man," whispered Marie.

She had never witnessed any of her Chippewa family's heathen rites. Like her, they knelt before the chancel rail in L'Arbre Croche, or bore the discipline of the missionary when he made his round of the islands. One solemn council she had seen, after the great chief Pontiac's war-token was first sent through the Northwest. Appeals of orators then rang among the trees. The sun shone on burnished bodies and arm-bands, and robes of beaver trailed the grass as majestic fellows trod back and forth in the passion of eloquence. This was to be a very different rite. The medicine-man stood with a wand in his hand, and his assistants measured and marked ground. Young Indians ran to cut saplings. Marie crept to the lodge door and drew the flap down, lest prying little Indian boys should seek her out, or their mothers try to make the lodge their refuge; and watched the whole plateau in front of her while she held the mat. Directly across that space walked Henry, with three Canadian boatmen at his heels. He was in the midst of the busy tribe before they saw him. Then their yell of exultation reverberated from island to island, and shook itself to silence far away in the east.

PART IV

THE HIGH PLATEAU

A HATCHET whizzed over the fire, making one revolution, and striking Henry's shoulder with the handle instead of the blade. A dozen mouths derided the marksman, and other hatchets were poised, when a huge old chief turned on his young men and stopped their sport. He had a stern aspect suited to the leader of the massacre at Fort Michilimackinac, and he was known to hate the English with a hatred scarcely less than Pontiac's. Henry remembered him as the Grand Sautor: the French called the Chippewa nation Sautors. He was an able political second to the master Indian mind of his day, and he would not now permit any action taken in his presence without first consulting the envoys from Detroit.

Henry stood in the midst of the savages, unconsciously affecting them by his presence.

They admired him. He had not dodged the hatchet. His shorn hair crisped in a gold fleece over his head. The flame in his eyes, they afterward said, burned holes in them.

When Marie saw him she sprang up in the closed lodge, but as the hatchet-handle struck him she dropped to her knees. He was not hurt. He stood alive among his enemies, and near her. Marie's body bloomed all over, the living smoothness of flower-petals enveloping her. The sun and summer, the world, and the meaning of life, returned, and she lived infinitely. Her blood buzzed in her ears. Whether we shall exist hereafter in a happier state, or run, shivering souls, a long gantlet of woes, there are instants here which compensate us for everything.

"—to give myself up," she heard Henry saying, as soon as she could hear anything.

One of his Frenchmen interpreted, turning from Henry to the Grand Sautor and from the Grand Sautor back to Henry as the talk proceeded. Masses of wrinkles around the old chief's eyes contracted in ironical scrutiny.

"Why is the Englishman such a fool as to come back and give himself up when he had escaped?"

"You know why," said Henry. "Because I cannot have any harm done to the chief Wawatam and his family."

"There stands the chief Wawatam. Who has threatened to do him or his family any harm?"

Wawatam stood with his shoulder toward Henry, lax and sullen in attitude.

"A message was sent to me that the tribe had disagreed about the present he made on my account, and if I escaped entirely they intended to burn him and his whole family."

"Who told you that?"

"The chief himself told it to a Pani woman that Mme. Cadotte bought at the fort."

"The chief lied."

Henry looked at Wawatam, a confused redness mounting in his face. "The chief never lied to me in his life."

There was silence among the Chippewas. The Detroit Indians had made use of the arts of war, and were at Michilimackinac to stir up recruits, but none of them answered Wawatam's grin as he raised his head. They knew that Henry was his adopted brother. It was a kind of betrayal which most nearly touched their religious natures.

"The Pani woman went with Mme. Cadotte in her boat, with the Englishman," said the Grand Sautor, examining evidence. "How could the Pani woman carry a message from the chief when she did not see him after the Englishman did?"

"She said he told her when I got into the boat, but forbade her to tell me before it was done, that if he did not give me up at the end of a week, the tribe would come over to the island and burn him and his family. As soon as we landed I persuaded Mme. Cadotte to let me take the canoe and some men and come back. The weather was against us. You have all come to the island as he said you would. What are you going to do?"

"It is none of the Englishman's business; but we came to consult the Great Turtle."

Henry saw the medicine-man and young Indians bringing a load of heavy poles for the mystic Turtle lodge. The evening fire burned harmlessly, little bead-eyed fellows huddling in copper nakedness between the blaze and their mothers' knees. Neither stake nor scaffold of torment appeared to have been thought of by the gathered multitude.

"My brother could have killed me while I was here," said Henry. "Why did he set a trap to bring me back?"

"Perhaps the Pani woman lied," suggested the Grand Sautor.

"The Pani woman did not lie," declared Wawatam, and he turned with a fierce stare at his English brother, the corners of his mouth drawn down, and the youthfulness of his face pitiably aged by deep creases. One week's debauchery had destroyed in him the civilization of two years. Race superiority in the other man still bore him down, and overrode his Indian weapon of treachery. He felt one of nature's wrongs. Henry listened in silence to what he had to say.

"My English brother's blood and mine were one. I hid him here, and gave him food; and he took what was mine away from me. I let him go out of my hand, but I fastened a cord to him. When he was gone, and I went to the black gown with my complaint, even the black gown was turned against me by English witchcraft, and would not let me have the wife promised to me. The black gown said: 'I will look into the matter. Perhaps it is best that no marriage take place between you and the French girl nourished in your grandmother's lodge.' If this man had not come back on account of the Pani woman's words, I would have followed him."

A deep breath was drawn by the listeners. They said, "Ho!" in admiration. Every English-hating breast acquitted Wawatam, and exulted in his craft.

"I did not take what he says was his," denied Henry, sternly. "That white islander who lives in his grandmother's lodge scarcely looked at me when I went away. If a priest would not marry her to him, neither would a priest marry her to me. She is too good for either of us."

"How many times did you see this French girl?" inquired the Grand Sautor.

"Only three times, when she came with a boy to bring my food, and helped build my lodge."

"Did Wawatam send her with food to the Englishman?"

Wawatam answered, "There was no one else to send, except the boy, who would forget."

The old chief looked at the young one with a grunt of contempt.

" Wawatam is a young man; he has learned nothing. And the black gown does not live among us to give or take away our women. Where is she now?"

Wawatam replied that she was probably in the woods with his grandmother, getting fuel; the lodge was empty.

"Did you not tell us that the Englishman took her from you?"

"He bewitched her. She would not go with me to L'Arbre Croche."

Squaws, watching the ivory whiteness and muscular beauty of the Anglo-Saxon, wondered how any woman could refuse to look at him. The Canadians were rabbits beside him, broad, brown-faced fellows, lacking that which comes and goes in power through the countenance.

"The English trader has come back and put himself in our hands," said the Grand Sautor, summing up facts. "What shall be done with him?"

Wawatam took a knife from his belt, but the old chief gave him a look which no young Chippewa ever disregarded. So deadly was the silent threat of the Grand Sautor that a European has set it down in letters—"The most undaunted person could not behold him without some degree of terror."

One of the Detroit envoys stepped between Henry and the Grand Sautor, and spoke against letting any Englishman live. Pontiac was strong enough, if all the tribes united with him, to sweep the English from the country. Wawatam's experience was common: wherever an Englishman went, he took everything, and pushed his red brother out·of his way.

When this speech was interpreted to Henry he understood why the Great Turtle was to be consulted. That esteemed and truthful spirit would tell the tribe whether a war against the English would be successful or not. The Chippewa nation hesitated after striking their first blow.

The impulse which brought Henry back to face these savages had not turned to indignation when he found himself made a fool of. He listened callously to gutturals on which his life hung, numb in the instinct of self-preservation. In the midst of the interpreting he was alert for a step or a rustle of leaves at the edge of the woods. Yet he did not own to himself what was working like madness in his cool English blood—that longing for the one beloved, which men laugh at, and die of, calling it by some other name. One or two happily nested birds cheeped from the oaks around the plateau, and the low call of an awakening owl came from the woods. The medicine-man, a disgusted practitioner, balked of his own importance, sat with his chin on his knees, waiting until the Englishman should be despatched. It was not for him to take the word out of the Grand Sautor's mouth, but when there was opportunity he hazarded the opinion that one Englishman less would neither gain nor lose the war; and popular conviction was with him.

"What have you to say for yourself?" inquired the Grand Sautor of Henry. "The English are no good, but we do not close their mouths."

Henry looked as relentlessly at his old enemy as that enemy looked at him.

"Why should I say anything? I felt obliged to come back, and I am here. You can do what you please with me now, though no Indian seemed able to kill me until trickery was used. But it is going to cost you dearly when you come to settle with the English, particularly Sir William Johnson."

At that name a wave of uneasiness passed through the camp. Sir William Johnson's influence extended from the valley of the Mohawk to the extreme northwest. He was the enemy of the French, but the manipulator and virtual lord of many eastern tribes. The Chippewas wished to be at peace with Sir William Johnson, at least until Pontiac's conspiracy was ripe enough for a successful sweep of the continent. But at Henry's implied threat the Grand Sautor rose up in defiance, and passed sentence.

"The Englishman came back to save his adopted brother from dying by fire. Even he saw that we had a right to burn somebody; and we will now use that right. The Englishman shall die by fire, that none of my people be disappointed."

Directly the camp was let loose. Ready braves seized Henry and pinioned his arms, while others tied his feet together. He felt grim amusement at being made so tame a victim in front of the wrinkled old idol, though escape or defense was impossible from the instant of his surrender.

"You fellows who have had my goods, and paid me no beaver, can pay me now," he remarked coolly.

The delinquents shouted when they understood him. They would pay him, indeed, with firebrands thrust into his ears, his eyes, and even down his parching throat. They would pay the whole English nation in him. Henry kept his feet, and looked at his adopted Chippewa brother.

Wawatam worked fiercely, digging the hole for the stake, driving in with his moccasined foot a spade which Henry had given him. Plenty of trees offered their trunks on every hand, but there must be space for the full enjoyment of roasting an Englishman, and the center of the open plateau, in front of the lodges, was the spot chosen. A pole intended for the Great Turtle's lodge was held by other Indians ready to be packed into its earthen socket. The world was then a deliberate world in all its corners; but the intoxication of haste which this continent produces worked even in aboriginal natures. It was not long before Wawatam withdrew his spade, and sullenly watched the muscles on bare backs crowding around the post, and many hands packing the dirt in. This was the only kind of planting to which an ambitious young Indian would degrade himself.

When Wawatam had walked through the woods guiding Henry to Mme. Cadotte's boat, he began to regret planning the Englishman's complete escape. He scarcely knew what he desired; but every step in their silent march was a step toward the end of friendship. At one moment the savage felt prompted to kill Henry in the woods, but the spiritual tie of Indian adoption still held. It was monstrous to hurt the person given to him by supernatural signs. If Marie would go to L'Arbre Croche and be married, it would be clear that Henry had done him no harm. If she would not, the story the Pani woman had told him, and the look he had himself seen, demanded revenge. They had reached the landing, and Wawatam saw the Pani woman in the boat with Mme. Cadotte before he hit on a scheme to bring the Englishman back. Henry might not respond to the test, or he might have to be concealed about the island again. Wawatam took all chances.

The young chief had told his hurt briefly

to his tribe. His own tongue failed to show all the change which had come over him. Little red tongues of fire springing from fat pine-wood should talk for him. And whatever counsel the Great Turtle might give, Wawatam was already decided; he had gone beyond his people in hostility to the English.

The most trivial incidents accompany the progress of death. Henry felt his sense of humor turn abnormally keen. The ludicrous side of the life he was about to leave affected him as a stimulant might have done. He saw George lying tipsy on Marie's bench, open-mouthed like a dead fish; and an old, hawk-faced Indian woman contentedly chewing her tongue while she rocked a child in the concave of her lap. He noticed a curious boy who tried to peep under the elbows of the earth-packers kicked end over end by the backward drive of a moccasin. Children as red as hairless puppies tumbled in a heap by the glowing log. The amenities of Indian life were being practised around Henry, and he fancied morsels of himself passed from hand to hand on a stick. It flashed across his mind like a vision that there are larger ways of doing things than any we know; that an archangel, for instance, might have managed this affair with honor, and without having a feather singed.

Henry's Canadian boatmen sat down by the fire, and took the chance to prepare themselves a little supper before camping elsewhere. They could not interfere with the political or personal revenges of a tribe, though their master would be sorry to hear that the Englishman was burned. Having brought him to the island, according to orders, they would rest a night before taking the boat back; but nobody could expect them to meddle with what happened in the Chippewa camp.

Sounds of chopping in the dusky woods seemed to reverberate along the edge of the sky. While some of the Indians cut fuel, others ran with arm-loads of it to build around the stake, which towered ten feet high, having the festive air of a May-pole. More than one knife would be stuck by cunning marksmen in the bark over the victim's head, and great sport it would be if every feint at throwing made him dodge. And when the hot air should rush upward as through a funnel, and the top of the pole begin to wave its little pennon of smoke, there would be no need of other light on the high level. The sky overhead was a delicate apple-green, one of those illusive tints which the crimson and orange of sunset leave in high northern air. Swarming figures became less and less distinct in outline, and darkness encroached from the woods, bringing sweet odors with it. Henry smelt the pine, and remembered his first night's plunge through the thickets of the island— the enchanted island, to which a man must come back though he come to his death.

As soon as their preparations were finished, the Chippewas dragged Henry to the stake and tied him. His bright head came up out of their buffeting, and steadied itself against the bark of the young tree. Through all his sensations he hoped that the presence of the Chippewas had driven Marie to some other part of the island for the night.

The wood was piled around Henry. Young Indians who had never seen a man burned stood by and learned cunning lessons in torture. The circle was not built as high as his knees; for a slow fire, steadily increased, would prolong the enjoyment of the camp far into the night.

Wawatam himself carried a brand from his outdoor hearth to light the pile. His eye and Henry's met as he knelt with the blazing pine. The Englishman's face was more distinct than Wawatam's. Not a word passed between them, and the barrier of flame began to rise, and separated them forever.

Some Indians who thought the spectacle needed illumination at its beginning were heaping wood on the camp-fire, and the crackle of the resinous fuel could be heard almost as far as its light could be seen. That shapeless black which we cannot call mere shadow, but people from childhood with monsters, drew away beyond the outermost trees. The ruby tinting of flame at night extended along the trampled sward, and up to oak twigs, seeming to edge the notchings of each leaf. The skins of naked babies grew roseate under this magic brush; and stilt-like shadows lay along the ground, mingling, and passing one another in constant caricature. Night was now overhead as well as around the little plane to which man's stature raises him; and stars were suddenly in their places, filmed with the light incense of burning wood.

The lodges, opaque and weather-beaten, were least responsive of any objects on the plateau. Stolidly they witnessed the threads of fire climbing around Henry's feet. The nearest lodge kept its secret of a French girl who had lain all of a summer night with his staff across her breast. It was silent and empty, the flap closing on its vacant hollow. For when the Indians seized Henry, Marie had snatched the blanket-gown at her bedhead, and torn an opening between mats at the back of the lodge. Her desperate rending shook the heavy structure. Any Chippewa beholder might have fancied the Great Turtle spirit already invoked, and in the throes of possessing the medicine-man. But the camp was in such an uproar that no one saw it, or Marie herself, when she broke through the hole and ran with her wool garment over her head to the nearest cover of trees.

She was leaving the open space behind, flying through the dead leaves, half bent to shoot under low-swung boughs, when she heard the Chippewa yell, and her flight became a deer's. Then a sound of chopping mingled with Indian exultation, and she knew there was no pursuit; the chief's young men were merely scattering to cut wood. Marie held both hands on her bursting heart, letting the blanket dress fall around her neck, and then around her waist, as her blood glowed and moisture broke through every pore.

A path made by prayerward feet to the rift in the island stretched its thread through the labyrinth of trees. She could not see far ahead in the darkness to which twilight sunk there, and the swish of leaves filled her ears. Headlong she ran against a man in a cassock, who caught her, and held her panting at arm's length. His white, benignant face was dimly visible. Brushing the twigs at a respectful distance behind him, other feet were coming, and Marie knew they were Noko's; she had counted on meeting the priest and the Indian grandmother in this path from the grotto chapel.

Marie leaned against a tree, dragging his hands. "Run, Father Jonois, to the lodges, and stop the Chippewas—forbid them to burn him!"

"To burn whom?"

"The Englishman, father. I broke through the back of the lodge. They are cutting the wood—I cannot speak!"

Her suffocating pulses hammered audibly, and the priest braced her against the tree with a grip which calmed. She tried to control her breath. Father Jonois spoke quietly.

"I saw canoes on the lake, and suspected mischief. I was coming to the lodges. The English trader escaped last week in Mme. Cadotte's boat. Why is he back on the island?"

"Because the chief sent him a message that we were all to be killed on his account. He gave himself up."

The wail in her voice told the priest all that he had vainly tried to learn concerning this Englishman while examining her conscience in the afternoon. She was reticent then, looking down, or at the sacred image in the niche, and speaking indifferently of all human beings. Father Jonois had made a trip to the island as soon as the straits were safe for his canoe-man, to satisfy his conscience in the matter of disposing of this young French girl.

"I will do what I can, my daughter. Are many of the Chippewas there?"

"Yes, father."

"Is the old chief with them?"

"Yes, father."

Father Jonois slightly shook his head. "Since this craze for war took them, they pay little attention to the priest."

He went swiftly forward on his new errand. Whether Father Jonois picked up his cassock and ran, or attendant spirits drew the bushes from his path, he was so excellent a footer of the wilderness that Marie could scarcely keep the darker blackness of his figure in sight. They left the Indian grandmother far behind, trudging under a load of bark and forest plunder. When the priest obliged Noko to go as far as the Virgin's chapel with Marie, and to receive religious prodding herself, she combined pleasure with discipline, and stole time from her prayers to forage among things which she better loved. It was hard to keep an old Indian woman facing toward an image on a rocky shelf while the rain-freshened woods invited her, and Father Jonois often let her drop her beads to go digging. She stopped many times to rest as night sifted on her in the thickets, chewing a cud of tender beech-mast or sassafras leaves, her nose and chin approaching and retreating, and her sighs of content stirring the silence which inclosed her. Chippewa yells, which shook echoes abroad from the open place where they were uttered, came to her muffled through much leafage. If she had seen the glare growing at the top of the island, it could have given no alarm to a householder with nothing to lose. Past the anguish of loving, of despairing, past the keen and useless cares of life, the happy old woman sat down in the woods and went to sleep.

No man was wiser in his day than a frontier missionary. He knew when to interfere, and when the tide of returning heathenism was too strong for him. Many a border family owed its safety to the restraining priest; and many another perished because even the confessional failed to give him all the clues to the dark hearts he labored for. Father Jonois had not been able to prevent the massacre at Michilimackinac, and the misery of that experience returned upon him as he mounted the plateau and saw the tall stake and its surrounding swarms. Wawatam was kneeling with his torch, and flames crept up the lattice of wood. Marksmen, bow in hand, were gathering at long range from the stake, and snaky eyes resented the black gown's appearance there. Wawatam shook the priest's hand from his wrist.

"You are lighting a fire to burn your own soul eternally," warned Father Jonois. "Put it out."

Wawatam stuck the brand into another place. Father Jonois began to tear down the pile with his naked fingers, and as many Chippewas as could seize him dragged him back from it. A few years earlier they might have killed him. But the religion of the black gown, even when it was disregarded, had now its established power.

Henry ground his teeth, the sweat of physical anguish and faintness moving in drops down his forehead. His face could be distinctly seen in the bold light. His arms were bound down against the smoking blanket-coat, but he had thrown it back from his neck before the Indians seized him, so that the beating pulses showed in the white brawn.

"It is not worth while to think of me," he called in French through the shimmering medium which separated him from the priest. "Think of the white islander, Monsieur Jonois, and take her away from this wretched tribe of savages."

He called Marie by the name he had given her instead of her own, which Wawatam might comprehend. This French girl, who never mingled with the tribe, but lived her secluded, happy life on the island, had been an object of unacknowledged superstition to the Chippewas. Not one of them laid a hand on her now as she flew from the woods and leaped into the circle of fire.

Her electrical muscles seemed to act without volition. She did not know what she was doing, but did it from foregone necessity, as a mother comes to the help of her child. The flower-like skin of her face was as stiff as a mask with the expressionless look of one meeting sudden death. The smoke swept sidewise, an inverted curtain, showing her dress of gull-breasts crisping to her body through every darkening plume, the ends of her braids and the little hairs edging them curling up. She had a woolen garment in her hand, and she wrapped it with her arms around Henry, and as she tried to protect him her face flamed with sweet helplessness and shame. The terrible weeping aloud of a hopeless woman pierced the roaring crackle of the fire. Father Jonois heard it with pangs which the massacre at the fort had not caused him.

But the sound, and Marie's touch with her poor little muffler, made Henry resplendent. All the beauty and strength of the man, all his physical endurance, and every endowment of tenderness, came upon him visibly as the power came upon Samson. He might have submitted alone to the torture of the Chippewas, and he knew there was no hope of escape; but he struggled until the cords of his arms cracked. The stake shook. He tore first one forearm and then the other from his thongs, and lifted Marie, shielding her face and head from the fire.

"Take her, Monsieur Jonois!" he shouted in French, and then in Chippewa to the Indians, "Let the priest go!"

But Marie herself held to the stake behind his head. Though she did not speak a word, he knew she was anchoring her fate to his, and would not be cast into safety.

"Then marry us!" Henry cried, and rapture deadened physical pain. In that delirium of heat and smoke he and the girl on his breast saw as a vision the life they might

have had together — their common hearth
and table, their days and nights of unbroken
companionship. Marie needed no mother to
tell her these things: the supplanter of
mothers is swift in teaching. Every part of
her which touched him said, "I love you."
She thought it like a prayer, "I love you."
Her breath came and went, a divine ether,
instead of the stifling fumes of burning wood,
carrying the one speechless fact which made
it worth the breathing — "I love you — I love
you."

The instant of Henry's breaking partly
loose was a breathless instant among the
Chippewas. But when he lifted Marie, and
flung his commands to priest and Indians,
Wawatam raised a yell. The quicksilver natures around the young chief responded.
They knew it meant instant and cruel death
to the Englishman and the French girl who
took up his cause. No time for torture, or
tickling a victim's ear, or stirring his hair
with well-planted arrows. The marksmen
dropped their bows, and ran to a carnival of
fire. Young braves stooped with Wawatam
to snatch brands or scoop live coals with
spade or bark platter or anything at hand

which would carry them from the campfire to heap on the two at the stake; and Father Jonois was beginning the marriage service.

A missionary adapted all his offices to the emergencies of life in the wilderness. These two asking marriage were of alien races, each knowing little of the other's past. He sincerely believed that one was doomed to perdition and the other required absolution instead of wedlock. Yet the Latin words rolled over his lips as at the command of heaven, for that cry out of the fire was a force as strong as religion.

The Chippewas holding the priest let him go, and ran after Wawatam. The nightmare which had lasted so long measured by pulse-beats, and so mere a point of time measured by the march of stars, was over before Father Jonois could further interfere. A man running across the open place with twenty strange Indians at his heels kicked the blazing wood from the stake, and scattered it with hands and feet as far as he could throw it. His deerskin boots smoked, and his face flamed with exertion. He cut Henry loose, two or three strokes of a knife dropping the

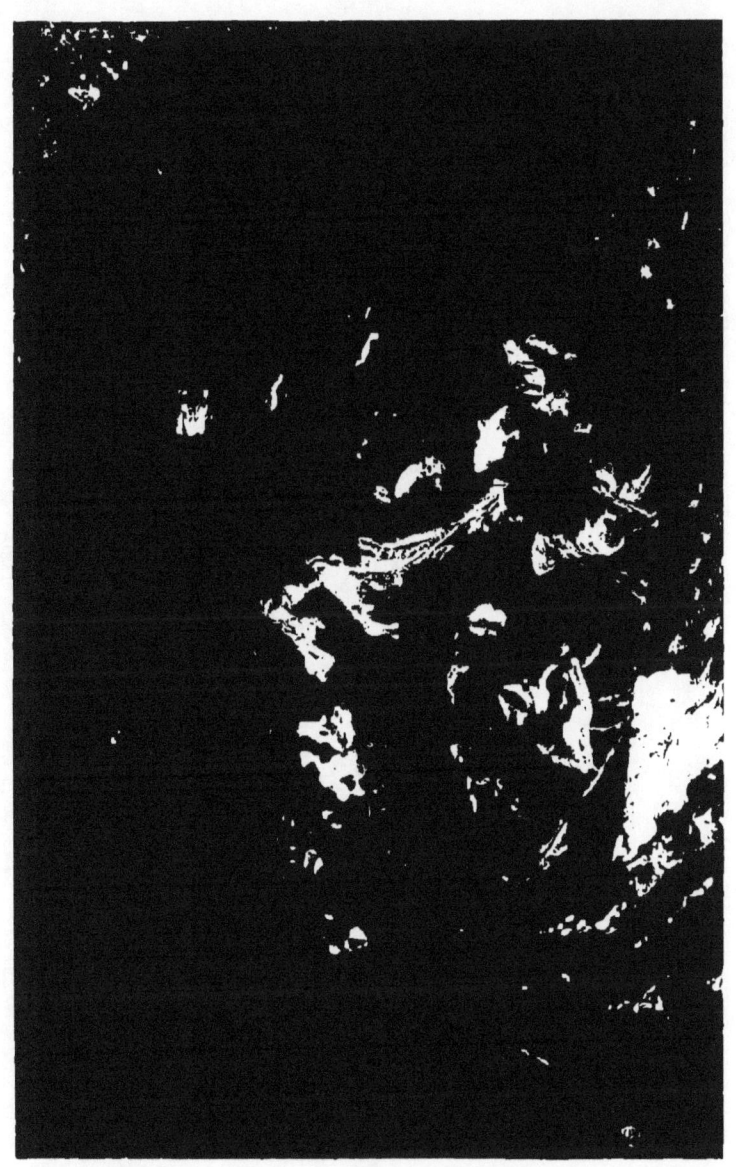

"FATHER JONOIS WAS BEGINNING THE MARRIAGE SERVICE."

thongs around the base of the post, and his men continued to tread out brands.

"Fools of Chippewas," he shouted, "what are you doing?"

Indians who had already lifted blazing pieces from the camp-fire, stood in a cluster like upright glow-worms; and others, shielding their faces and plucking, were startled in the act. They would have risen knife in hand against any other white man in the Northwest who assumed such authority over them; but M. Cadotte was not only their friend,—he had married into their tribe,—he was also the lord of all the red villages around Sault Ste. Marie. They knew his influence had kept the Lake Superior Indians from joining Pontiac, and their own pause since lifting the hatchet had resulted from that knowledge.

As the blaze around the stake was quenched, darkness again encroached upon the plateau from the woods, though one by one brands were dropped back on the camp-fire. Patches of creeping redness, where smoke was just breaking into sullen flame, showed on Henry's woolen clothes. M. Cadotte pulled off his coat and the priest took his cassock skirts to smother them, and Marie was stripped of her heated blanket-cloth, from which the sewed feathers dropped like burnt gum. Sudden terror of herself as an inflammable material made her submit to have the smoldering dress torn off by Father Jonois, and he shoved her through the half darkness into her lodge.

The night wind, flowing from the lakes across mossy forests cooled by a week's rain and moist with freshly condensed dew, was sweet after that hot breath of torment. It came to Marie through the hole she had made between the mats, and she threw herself on the ground as she had often thrown herself in the lake water, prostrate before the good God who drenched her with such joy.

The Chippewas drew together at the camp-fire, red light shining between their moving legs. Their brutal carnival died out as quickly at M. Cadotte's shout as it had arisen with Wawatam's yell. He noticed when he approached them that the young chief Wawatam was gone. M. Cadotte was too well skilled in treating with Indians to look around the dark edges of the camp apprehensively, but the fact that Wawatam might be skulking made him say briefly what he had to say. The crimson stack of reviving brands gave him a ruddier hue than was natural, though he was a hale, well-built Frenchman, dark-haired, and very animated in gesture.

"And have you been sitting here, Grand Sautor, and allowing your young men to destroy their nation?" he inquired, confronting the old image.

The Grand Sautor made no reply, but waited to hear what had happened at the Sault to make M. Cadotte take all this trouble for an Englishman. Some little satisfaction embedded itself in his wrinkles that the Englishman was at least well scorched before being turned loose. The medicine-man, resting his horns against a tree, relaxed in weary disgust. He knew the Great Turtle spirit would not be consulted that night.

"As many burns as there are on that young Englishman's body, that many Chippewas will Sir William Johnson have for them. What! Do you not know that this man is his relative? I would not have let the young Englishman come back if I had been at the Sault when he arrived. But I was away, meeting messengers sent from Fort Niagara, from Sir William Johnson. He sent for his young relative. And he has come as far as Fort Niagara to meet the tribes of the Northwest. His kettles are hung, full of meat. The messengers said he intended to load your canoes with powder and shot and blankets, and more presents than you can carry away. Are you so fond of your old bows and arrows for hunting when you can have firearms? What will he say when I am obliged to tell him, 'Monsieur, these fools of Chippewas have listened to evil birds from Detroit and other places, and have put your young relative into the fire?'"

M. Cadotte turned abruptly on the sullen Detroit envoys sitting with their knees up to their chins.

"Did these fellows tell you that Detroit is taken? Detroit is not taken. It never can be taken. The St. Lawrence River is black with canoes, and the canoes are full of English soldiers. Pontiac cannot stand against such power. And here are you — laying up crimes against the lives of your women and children! Will you go to this council at Fort Niagara, and make peace with a people who have you in their hands? I am of your tribe, and I see nothing else for us to do. Or will you refuse? The messengers wait at the Sault, and you must come and tell them yourselves what you will do."

Marie had not finished changing her moccasins and girding on one of her blanket-gowns when Father Jonois called her. She hung her beads in her girdle, and tied her birch-bark cap under her chin. There was nothing else for her to take. She looked back at her wilderness nest. Noko's vacant bed gave her a pang. She had forgotten the old grandmother. Noko must be dozing somewhere on the path, under a load of bark and roots. What would she do when she trudged home to the lodges and found no French girl ready to take off her load and ladle her belated supper out for her?

"O dear Noko!" said Marie.

But the sweet necessity of going where her love went hurried her out of the little home, and she dropped the flap forever behind her.

The camp-fire, coaxed by the squaws, was lifting candle-flames and making the plateau flicker. Those faces which had always been strange to Marie, distantly watched her now, half sinister in their wordless scrutiny. M. Cadotte had his Canadians and Indians mustered, and he surrounded the Englishman with them. It was necessary to hurry to the boats. The fluctuating aboriginal temper which he had turned toward peace might turn back toward war the next minute, reckless of consequences. And the young chief Wawatam, who had separated himself from the savage bivouac, might work harm with arrows in the darkness which the following council would never be able to mend. M. Cadotte was sincerely attached to his Chippewa relatives.

"But where is George?" said Marie. "Can we not take him along?"

"No, no; it would not do," objected M. Cadotte. The Frenchman had no mind to make a further breach with Wawatam by abducting his adopted son.

Marie paused at the bench where George lay, and put her hand on his unconscious head.

"O poor George! Who will take care of him?"

"Make your mind easy, my child," said Father Jonois. "I will look after George."

"But some one must drive him to bathe, Father Jonois, or he would not wash himself once a year."

"I will lay it upon him as penance," promised Father Jonois; "as indeed it is to most of my flock."

"O George, the saints also watch over you," whispered Marie; and George stirred in his heavy sleep, bubbling half articulately:

"All good."

Then, understanding what she risked by pausing, Marie hurried down the familiar path to the bay through the moist, sweet woods. Indian-pipes were perhaps springing about her, parting dead leaves as they shot like rising souls above the earth. Would there fail a girl to search them out and love them while the island stood on the waters?

Her island—her dear island!

And then she remembered the chief who had been kind to her two years. But Henry held her hand against his breast as they walked. She felt the pang of all his burns, and knew that every eye kept watch on thickets ahead; and it puzzled her that our good and evil are so mixed in this world that we cannot separate them.

"For what could I not have done to the Pani woman," flashed through Marie's mind, "if the Pani woman had this hand which now holds mine? The poor chief cannot know it was impossible for me ever to go to L'Arbre Croche with him."

SOUTH of the Cheneaux islands there was a redness in the east which surprised the eye like dawn at night, until a disk appeared, inflamed and pushing upward. It was the old moon, diminished in figure, but grand, as the lady of the sky forever is. As the flush died away, woods, islands, and immense stretches of water sprung to distinctness in her mystic day, and she unrolled her web of tapestry along the rippling pavement below. There was no more than a ripple on the straits.

Father Jonois's canoe moved away from the little fleet heading toward the Sault. He had just finished the sacrament of marriage and his admonitions to the bridegroom, while the Canadians held the boats together in mid-channel. A problem that had troubled him two years was now solved, and his conscience acquitted him of the French girl whom her husband called the white islander. In winter he used to cross the ice on a sledge to make sure she was well and happy with her Chippewa household, and he guarded her at all seasons in the semi-savage lot from which she sprung into beauty. She loved him with veneration; yet she had just kissed his hand and turned away to the uttermost parts of the earth with a stranger she had never seen when that moon was new.

"There are women," thought the priest, "who have a vocation for loving as plain as others have for the holy life."

His expert canoe-man, who had ventured on more than one perilous journey with him, looked forward to an easy night crossing. Widening triangles of light showed behind the eastward-moving boats as they clove the water. An auroral play of camp-fire could be seen on the summit of Mackinac above the white cliffs and foliage dome. Night had never seemed less savage on that coast. Father Jonois, turning his back on accomplished duty and visible things, began to whisper prayers. Still a glamourous influence, as resistless as music, stole out from that island, and followed the canoe while it pushed its breastplate of foam toward sparks of French windows at Fort Michilimackinac.

www.ingramcontent.com/pod-product-compliance
Lightning Source LLC
Chambersburg PA
CBHW031447160426
43195CB00010BB/894